Hunting for Antiques and Collectables

The Adventures of an Antique Collector

Dr Giora Ram

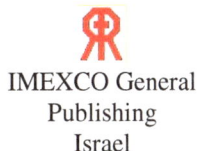

IMEXCO General
Publishing
Israel

Books by Dr Giora Ram

ADHD - Children of Tomorrow
Published in Israel by 'Gvanim' - [2010]
http://adhd.imexco.com - DanaCode 0-00860000644-6

The House on the Hill
Published in Israel by IMEXCO General Ltd - [2010]
Poems and Love Letters
http://love-u.imexco.com - DanaCode 0-08000250081-4

My Love, My Wife, My Divorcee
Published in Israel by IMEXCO General Ltd - [2010]
Dating and Mating
http://my-love.imexco.com - DanaCode 0-08000250082-1

The Hungarian Connection
Published in Israel by IMEXCO General Ltd - [2010]
An Autobiographical Novel
http://huncon.imexco.com - ISBN 978-965-91623-0-7 (Amazon)

Sex and Scientific Philosophy
Published in Israel by IMEXCO General Ltd - [2012]
A unique collection of earthly and heavenly questions arising during our intellectual evolution.
http://philosex.imexco.com - ISBN 978-965-91623-1-4 (Amazon)

Copyright © 2013 by the Author

First published in Israel by IMEXCO General Ltd.

All rights reserved. No part of this publication may be reproduced, stored in a retrieval system, or transmitted, in any form or by any means, electronic, mechanical, photocopying, recording, or otherwise without the prior permission of the copyright holder.

Printed in Israel

ISBN 978-965-91623-2-1
http://antiques.imexco.com

Contents

1. Prologue — 5
2. The Philosophy of Negotiation — 9
3. The King and I — 21
4. The Hungarian Findings — 24
5. The Great Discovery in India — 29
6. From Russia with Love — 31
7. Auctions and Fairs in England — 36
8. Judaica — 40
9. Made in Palestine and Israel — 51
10. Wooden Made Items — 60
11. Porcelain and Pottery — 68
12. Islamic and Persian Antiques — 75
13. Desktop Collectables — 80
14. Tobacciana and Boxes — 89
15. Coins and Medals — 100
16. Jewellery and Watches — 104
17. Flatware and Kitchenware — 110
18. Paintings, Prints and Photography — 121
19. Asian Art — 129
20. Furniture, Carpets and Lighting — 134
21. General Antiques and Collectables — 138
22. Epilogue — 144

If you wish to persuade me, think my thoughts, feel my feelings and speak my words (Cicero).

1. Prologue

The word antiques usually refers to the obvious meaning of an old collectable item. In Latin *antiquus* means old. There are many reasons for such an item to be collected. It is desired because of its rarity, beauty, workmanship, usage or certain emotional or unique features.

In order for an object to be classified as an antique, it should be at least a hundred years old. If an item is less than a hundred years old, it might be called *collectable* and may be the antique of tomorrow. This definition is adopted by custom offices worldwide and is used in legal terminology for antiques.

The first chapter is about the philosophy of negotiation and it is based on the author's negotiation skills and experiences in his international business endeavours.

Particular experiences, especially regarding antique markets, are included.

In Tel Aviv, the author indulged in his hobby by attending the local antique market every Friday, not only as a buyer, but also as a seller.

The monetary reward was insignificant and often did not cover the expenses and fees involved in participating in the market as a regular dealer, but he very much enjoyed the atmosphere, and his encounters with a diversity of people, both collectors and dealers.

The author is a world traveller, who has visited many places, especially those where tourists never go. His adventures have taken him to unusual locations, markets and auctions worldwide.

Some of the unique and rare items found during those trips are described here. The collectable and antique items in this book are part of the entire collection owned and photographed by the author. They are displayed at: http://antiques.imexco.com

The items on the *Antiques Online Catalogue* website are constantly updated and displayed in the following main categories:

Israeliana and Judaica - This category contains the following items: Candelabra, Hanukkah and Menorah Lamps, Spice Boxes and Towers, Torah Pointers, Etrog (Esrog) Boxes, Kiddush Cups and Goblets, Megillah Scrolls, Bezalel and related items, Wooden Ware, Pal-Bell, Teppich items and general Judaica collectables.

Metal Ware - Here we have a diversified collection of metal made items such as: pitchers, pots, flatware, hollow ware and general metal collectables, some made of sterling silver, silver plated, pewter and other metallic alloys.

In this category, we have a special section for kitchenware, items we use on our dining tables such as: salt and condiment holders and shakers, napkin rings, serving flatware, tongs, ladles and tea related items.

Ethnic and Cultural Antiques - In this category, we have typical and rare items from around the world such as: Imperial Russian items, Asian Art, Inro, Netsuke, Ivory and other sculptures, Middle-Eastern Islamic unique Copper and Brass Ware with Inlaid Silver.

Desktop Collectables - Here we present items used on office and home desks such as: inkwells, letter openers, pens and pencils and other desktop related collectables.

Tobacciana - In this category, we have in addition to the classical tobacciana collectables, such as pipes and related items, but also cigarette and snuff boxes, mainly made of silver, as they are highly collectable.

Jewellery and Watches - Diverse, simple, and low cost jewellery items such as: bracelets, brooches, pins, compacts, earrings, necklaces, pendants, rings are presented here. In addition, certain watches and antique chains are also included in this category.

Photography - In addition to the cameras and photographic related equipment; we may see unique antique Tintypes – Ferrotype photographs starting from the 1860s and Carte De Visite - CDV from the1870s.

Coins and Medals - General coins and medals, mainly from Israel, are presented here. A few Roman and Hasmonean are coins are also included. These coins are genuine ancient Roman bronze coins from 230 BCE and up to the 4th Century CE. They were discovered and auctioned in Israel.

Painting and Prints - Paintings, prints, lithographs, etchings, engravings and drawings are displayed in this category of art.

Furniture and Carpets – Antique and vintage furniture are displayed with carpets, rugs and lighting ware.

Music and Records - Musical instruments and antique records are displayed in this category.

In addition to the above main categories, there are other general collectables and many are displayed on the *Antiques Online Catalogue* website.

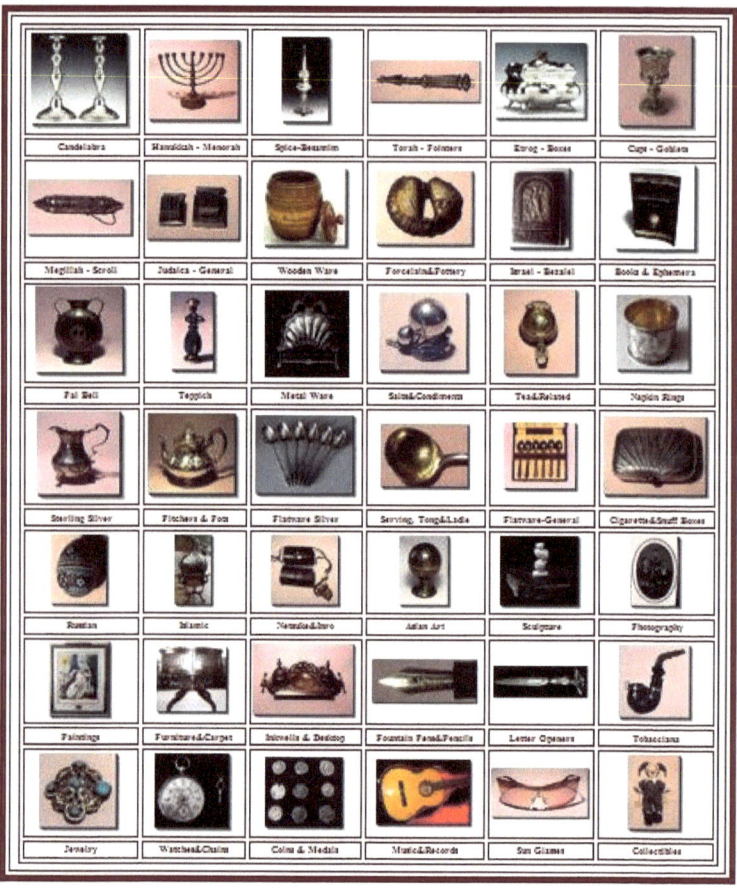

The author has decided to adopt and implement the saying:

A picture is worth a thousand words.

Accordingly, the emphasis in this book is on pictures, rather than on words (430 colour pictures).

A reader who wishes to inquire and learn more about an item in this book, may do so by either visiting the website mentioned above, or by searching the Internet.

Dr Giora Ram, 2013

2. The Philosophy of Negotiation

It is fair to say that we have been negotiating since birth. We started as children, negotiating with our parents, family and friends.

When we were given options such as 'if then else', we tried to improve the conditions by negotiating a better deal. Occasionally, we even negotiated with ourselves.

Our ancestors negotiated with God at the creation and later with everybody else. We have improved and expanded our negotiating skills and today they are widely applied, not only known and practised by attorneys. Negotiations are conducted in diverse arenas, each requiring different negotiation skills, but we can find commonalities among them.

We need to negotiate with terrorists, kidnappers and bank robbers, where the outcome can be deadly, and we may save lives if we succeed.

We negotiate in shops and markets, where no sale is the worst case scenario.

There are mild and aggressive negotiations. We negotiate contracts for buying and selling and 'if then else' is one of the basic elements in negotiation.

One-sided ultimatum negotiation is common as well, such as: 'These are my terms', 'Take it or leave it' and 'It's not negotiable'.

The philosophy of negotiation takes into account that the parties are interested in executing a common deal.

Each party, however, sets certain standards, conditions and limits which they will accept or agree to.

For example, A has certain goods for sale and B is interested in purchasing. Here are several scenarios:

1. The goods have a fixed price set by A, like drugs in a pharmacy or goods in certain stores. B has no negotiating options; either he agrees to the price and buys the goods, or refuses to pay the asking price and goes shopping elsewhere.
2. The goods have a fixed price set by A, but there might be a special discount. The discount may be subject to submitting previously published coupons or based on certain conditions, such as store membership or seasonal sale. In this case, the buyer is given a conditional or unconditional price discount, but without negotiating options.
3. The goods have a fixed price set by A. The price caters for a certain discount, based on the buyer's negotiating skills. Buyer B has the option to offer a lower price and A in return may either accept or make a counter offer, until they reach agreement; otherwise there is no deal.

We will analyse a general negotiation case between seller A and buyer B.

The obvious goal of A is to sell for the highest possible price, and the opposite goal of the buyer is to pay the minimum price. The assumption is that both are willing to enter into the negotiation phase to conclude the deal.

We will try to understand the philosophy behind their thoughts and strategies for optimally achieving their goals.

The seller knows that he is entering into a negotiation arena and accordingly has embedded in the asking price a certain acceptable discount margin.

In his mind, the seller may have set a minimum price that he would accept, and below that minimum there will be no sale.

A has set his asking price at $100, but he realizes that the chance to sell at the asking price is quite slim. He has set a minimum selling price a priori at $60.

Buyer B may have similar thoughts. She knows that the asking price has a certain amount of discount, which is subject to negotiation. Therefore, she decides not to agree to the asking price of $100. In her mind, she decides to pay a maximum of $80.

Seller A encourages buyer B to make an offer. B tries a 'fishing trip' and provocatively offers only $50.

Hearing the ridiculous offer, A overcomes his inclination; he wants to sell, but will not accept $50 and he responds with a counter offer of $80.

B is hooked now, as she realizes that the new offer is the price she is willing to pay. Although she may have the option to end the negotiation by accepting the new offer, B as an experienced negotiator makes another attempt and offers to pay $60.

Seller A realizes that they have reached the sum he is willing to accept; he has the option to terminate the negotiation as well, but A is also an experienced negotiator so he uses the 'meet them halfway' system. This is a classical negotiation method, where both parties want the deal and each thinks that the middle of both offers is a fair way to close the deal. The parties agree the deal and the negotiation closes for $70.

In this case both parties are happy, the buyer who thought she would have to pay $80 got the goods for only $70, less than she expected, and at the same time the seller, who thought he would be willing to sell for $60 actually received more than he anticipated.

A good and a fair deal is when both parties end up happy with their decisions. Both parties made their optimal choices and both will leave the negotiation with a winning feeling.

Obviously, this is the ideal scenario and it has many different endings in terms of the closing price or in walking away from the deal.

In an auction sale, the final price is set by the auctioneer's hammer and no direct negotiation is possible. The process of bidding from the starting price until the hammer comes down involves a lot of psychology, however.

Potential buyers are bidding, or more precisely fighting, among themselves, in order the get the item they desire.

Often they are carried away by their emotions and pay more than they decided a priori to pay, or even more than they can afford. The auction hall is the ground for the hunt.

Ego, usually male ego, is one of the parameters which will decide a final price many times above market value or the buyer's real need.

'There is a cheaper item over there', said the potential buyer to the seller. The seller asked for $100 and the buyer said: 'But over there, they asked only $70'. The seller replied: 'OK, so buy it there'. The buyer said: 'But they have sold it already'. The seller said: 'Thanks for the info, so now my price is $120'.

Another version might be: 'So why don't you buy it over there?'. The buyer: 'Unfortunately they have sold their entire inventory'. Seller: 'OK, when my inventory runs out, I'll sell it for only $50'.

Pricing is a science with a lot of psychology. When the price is too high, people will not buy; too low a price is not only loss of extra profit for the seller but it is not appreciated by the buyer.

Cheap is cheap

Pricing is affected among others by context and location. The same item sold in a market, in a small shop or in a boutique in an affluent neighbourhood can make a significant difference in price. Price is obviously affected by the uniqueness and the rarity of the item.

A rare nineteenth-century silver and enamel object made by Fabergé may fetch a significantly higher price than a similar item made elsewhere in another period by an unknown maker.

In an open trading market environment, price is often not displayed or fixed by the seller. Experienced sellers do not label products with a price if they are willing to negotiate. They will however make an ad hoc decision, based on buyer's image, origin, sex and other factors and set the initial asking price accordingly.

It is interesting to observe the diverse negotiation skills and methods deployed worldwide.

There is culture-oriented negotiation such as in the Middle East, where there is a significant gap between the asking and the final selling price.

Price may be affected by the gender of both the seller and the buyer, whether he or she is local or a tourist and even by appearance, smell, voice and other factors.

Don't ever bid against yourself

If you as the seller have set an asking price, do not start to change it when you see and feel that the buyer is not interested. If the buyer is truly interested, s/he will enter into the negotiating arena. In this case, if you lower your initial asking price, you will lose the starting negotiation point. Ask the buyer to make the first counter offer to your first asking price. This case is clearly demonstrated in the example described above.

The more you seem to be eager to sell the less you'll succeed

Do not run after buyers, play it cool. In most cases, you cannot persuade a potential buyer to buy if s/he is not interested. The buying and selling possibilities available on online trading websites such as eBay are: *fix, auction, make an offer* or *buy it now.*

The 'fix' price is the situation of 'take it or leave it' with regard to the indicated fixed price.

The 'auction' option requires one buyer to bid for the starting auction price and it may increase if other bidders are interested to buy; eventually the highest bidder wins.

In the 'make an offer' option, the seller enables the buyer to make an offer. In this case, the seller may accept the offer or make a counter offer, until they reach an agreement.

The 'buy it now' option may be combined with the 'auction' option, whereby the buyer may bid and compete with other potential bidders, or accept the 'buy it now' price and win immediately.

Negotiation skills are required in conflict management, arbitration, conflict resolution and mediation. If A has a conflict with B and A is our client, the best advice to A is to bring a third party C into the equation.

This may yield a stronger and a better result. By bringing C into the conflict, we consider future situations and relations that might evolve after the negotiation is terminated. It holds true especially in cases where A has to continue personal or business relations with B.

Negotiation is quite often seen as confrontation. Effective negotiations need not be confrontational, however. Setting the mood as aggressive and seeking to win means that there must be a loser.

The correct attitude of the opposing parties should not be to win the confrontation but to find a mutually agreeable solution.

It is necessary to control our emotions during the negotiation process. The more we lose control and become emotional, the less we will be able to achieve an efficient, desirable and mutually agreed solution.

We must make an effort to focus on the issues in hand and not on the specific and sometimes annoying personality of our counterpart. Blaming the other side is a definite distraction and an unproductive one.

One of the most important factors in efficient negotiation is to research and understand the needs of the other party.

To find a mutually agreeable solution to the problem, we need to assess the gap between our needs and any disagreements. We will be able to do so only after understanding the needs and worries of our opponent.

A typical example of how such understanding can be effective is the following scenario. Let us assume that two people have found a coconut and each is claiming it should be theirs.

You happen to be there and you are chosen to be the arbitrator. What would be your ultimate solution to this conflict?

Most of arbitrators would simply suggest splitting the coconut in half. In this case each claimant will have only 50% of what they want. Is it the best ultimate solution? Well, not really.

If you had talked first to each party to learn their needs before making your ruling, you might have found out that one of them is an artist interested only in the coconut shell for carving, whereas the other just wanted the milk and the coconut meat.

With this information you would be able to satisfy 100% of each party's needs and reach a classical win-win situation.

Timing is everything. Negotiations, like many other things in life, are time-dependent. There are better and worse times and places to conduct negotiations. When entering into the negotiation process, we should be prepared, learn about our opponent, prepare alternative solutions, not waste time on futile arguments, never get emotional and present persuasive arguments to support our claims. Essentially, the aim of negotiation is to cause a change in our opponent's perspective that may lead him/her to agree and come closer to our needs and desires.

A good and efficient negotiator is one who has the ability to persuade. Sometimes a negotiator needs to use his/her persuasive skills for the sole purpose of encouraging the parties to open up, to talk, to listen and to start a dialogue.

There are many persuasion techniques that are used by negotiators. Some are positive and some are negative. Among the positive techniques are basic physical touch and gestures like handshake, smile, compliments, respect and other small-talk to generate a certain atmosphere of familiarity.

The negative attitude used in the persuasion process may contain obvious or hidden threats such as 'if then else'. Monetary threats are usually very effective tactical methods, especially in financial arguments. Failing is another negative technique, and can be considered as a major psychological punishment. Therefore, when entering into the negotiation process, we should set aside our fear of failing or losing.

One of the basic and most primitive human motivators is fear. The fear of losing property, wealth, a game or anything else puts us in a weak position in the negotiation process.

We should try to control and monitor our non-verbal signals. Our body language sends out revealing messages, especially when we are angry, frustrated or eager to accept and agree to a proposal or to a compromise.

In our daily life we face conflicts that require negotiation in order to resolve them. A typical example is conflict between employees and employers, Employees want more money and better working conditions and employers want to make more profit and minimize their labour costs.

In certain countries and in specific cases, employees are united under a local labour union responsible for the actual negotiation with the employer. Such negotiation will normally take several rounds of meetings, in which different scenarios emerge.

There are cases where the union may demand certain changes, such as salary increases. There are several negotiation styles and methods that can be used either by the union or the employees acting independently.

They may enter the negotiation arena with an ultimatum such as: 'If then else…' or alternate demands and response may take place between employees and employer.

Experienced negotiators will add to the basic minimum demands an extra demand or several demands that will be given up later, as an act of goodwill, so that not all demands will be met.

Consequently, at the end of the process, both sides may declare themselves the winner. This mutually agreed compromise is essential for the ongoing relationship between the parties as they have to continue to work together.

In an aggressive ultimatum environment, employees must understand perfectly the philosophy and the needs of management, as they might not react well to an ultimatum. This holds true especially in cases where the employer is seeking a way to close the business, replace certain employees or perform reorganization.

Employers may use this ultimatum situation to resolve their business problems and get rid of trouble-makers.

Here are several scenarios between union and employer:

Union: 'We want a 20% salary increase'.
Employer: 'No way!'.
Union: 'OK, so what about 10%?'.

Such an early retreat by the union obviously signals to the employer that they are weak and they may end up with no or a small salary increase of maybe 5%.

Union: 'We demand 20% salary increase, otherwise we quit'.
Employer: 'OK, so quit'.

In this case the union were not prepared for such a response and they are now faced with the problem of how to proceed.

If the employer is just testing how far they are willing to go, there might be some room for compromise.

If, however, the employer is serious about closing the business or replacing certain employees, then the union may have caused irreversible damage to the employees.

Union: 'We demand a 20% salary increase. Our demand is based on the increase in the company's profit made during the last two quarters. This profit was enabled as the result of the extraordinary dedication, extra hours and production improvements of the employees. Moreover, in order to make it more acceptable, we are willing to accept this increase in two instalments'.

This is a reasoned claim by the employees and it is probable that the management will accept the principle and agree to some or even all of their demands.

Employer: 'As a result of your inability to supply the ordered goods on time, we lost our client. This caused substantial financial damage and I have to make a certain reduction in labour. You the union must supply the names of ten employees to be fired'.

Union: 'We understand the need but not the means to resolve the problem. We suggest that we do not fire those ten employees, but agree to make up the equivalent cost in salary reduction. This reduction will be in effect until the company is back in track. When the company is profitable again, we ask that the employees are remunerated with that salary reduction plus a bonus'.

In this case a reasonable employer would accept such an offer, as the benefit in the long run is obvious. The chief asset of any company is its employees. In this case they want to stay, accept a salary reduction and make an effort to succeed and put the company back on track.

The union was very clever to make such an offer. No employees will be fired. The loss in salary reduction may become a good investment for the future. Not only will employees get that amount back, but they will receive an additional bonus as well. It is almost a win-win situation.

Time-dependent negotiation is when employees enter negotiation after or during a strike, while the business has to deliver certain goods already paid for, for example. Each day of the strike costs the employer money and they are unable to deliver the goods they might well lose the order.

In such a case, the employer may have a monetary interest in ending the strike as early as possible and the employees know that. They also know that if they fail to deliver the goods in time they might lose their jobs. In such a case, both parties have an interest in ending the dispute as soon as possible and both realize that they have to compromise.

Both employer and employees can evaluate and calculate their win or lose time-dependent costs. The balance in most cases is somewhere in between the demands and the offers of the parties involved. Delaying the compromise or stopping the strike can be beneficial or advantageous to either party or to neither.

Obviously, there are many more variations of employer-employee relationships and they may contain many different elements depending on the type of business conducted.

Employers' dependence on employees in a high-tech company is different from that on employees in a purely service-oriented company; the first have vital information about the company's products, whereas the latter can be replaced without loss of knowledge.

Replacing a high-level engineer is more difficult than replacing a hotel bellboy. Such a dependency plays a major role in the negotiation between the parties concerned.

A business structure where certain key employees hold the management hostage by threatening to leave or go to the competition may put the management in a weak negotiating position. The case may be even worse when those key employees hold exclusively the know-how technology.

The above-mentioned negotiation scenarios are applicable in certain cases to disputes between countries as well.

In summary, negotiation is a dialogue between two or a group of people.

The main intention is to reach an agreement and understanding or to resolve conflicts between the parties.

It is essential that the parties enter into the negotiation phase willingly and that they commit to accept and execute the resulting outcome. Normally, a good negotiation process is terminated by a compromise acceptable to both sides.

The definition of a good negotiating process, however, is not when one side wins but when all negotiating parties come out as winners. This can happen only when a win-win situation is achieved.

What does it take to persuade people? How does a lawyer cause an arbitrator, judge, businessperson or other lawyer to reach the desired conclusion of their own volition?

> *If you wish to persuade me, think my thoughts, feel my feelings and speak my words* (Cicero).

3. The King and I

Hussein bin Talal was the King of Jordan. King Hussein was seeking if there was any way to resolve the dispute with Israel peacefully. His secret meetings with the Israelis were held in London and in many other places during the period of 1963 to 1994 when the Israeli-Jordan Treaty of Peace was signed.

One of those meetings was with the Israeli Foreign Minister Ehud Barak at the Royal Palace in Amman. Barak met with King Hussein, with whom he had a warm relationship, in January 1996, to brief him on the latest developments concerning the Syrian-Israeli peace talks.

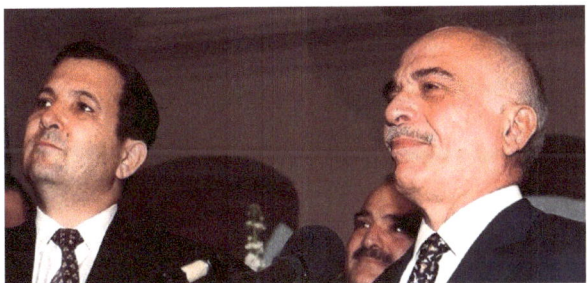

The King was known to give special gifts to certain visitors, and during one of those meetings, he gave Ehud Barak a unique coffee set, which was made of sterling silver, inlaid with gold and Limoges porcelain, held by silver cups, all bearing the King's mark. The sterling parts were made in Germany, almost 3Kg silver in a quality large velvet box.

The Administrator General from the Israeli Ministry of Justice is in charge when relating to the receipt and administration of all property bestowed on Israel. In the case of non-monetary gifts, such as real estate, securities, objects d'art or other valuable items, the Administrator General sees to their sale, and the transfer of the monies received to Israel.

Accordingly, that coffee set was auctioned and I bought it.

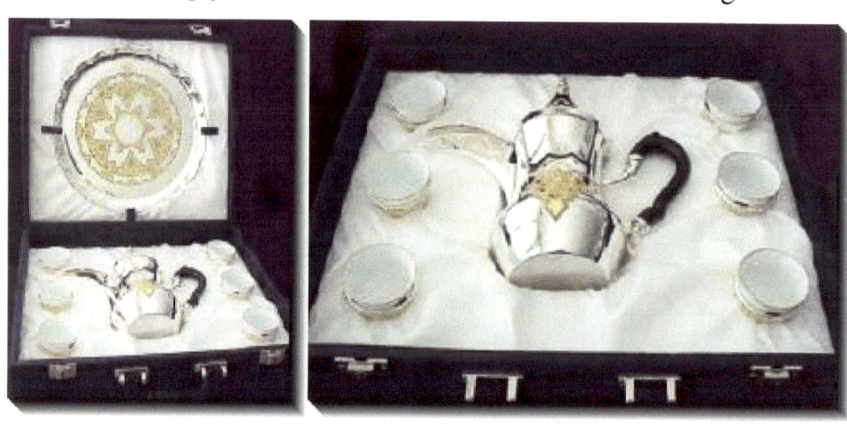

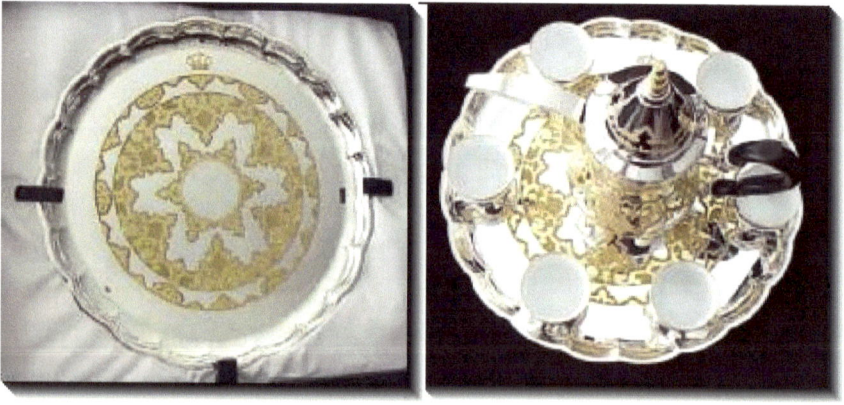

The porcelain Limoges parts were made by Bernardaud, France.

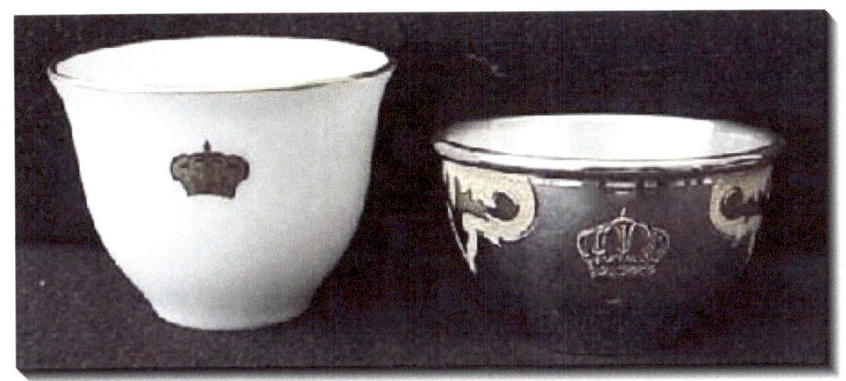

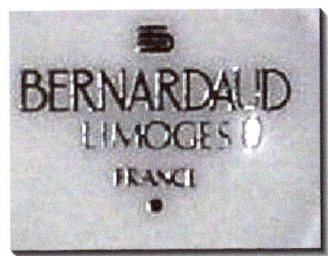
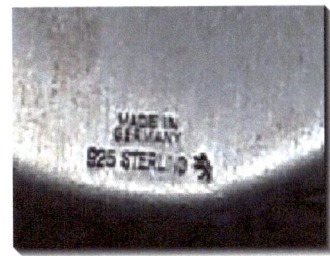

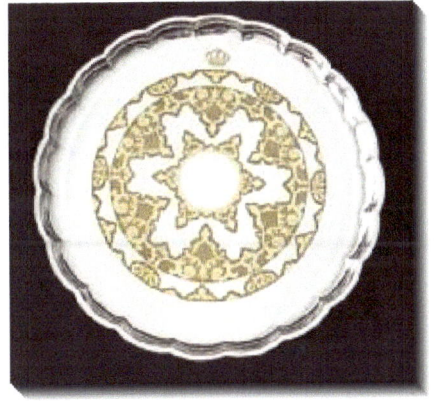
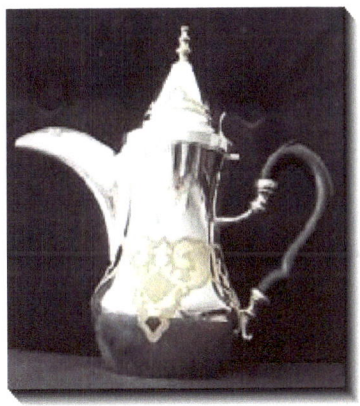

4. The Hungarian Findings

This Kiddush Cup was bought by my mother and her sisters on July 7th 1935 to commemorate my Grandparent's forty years of happy marriage.

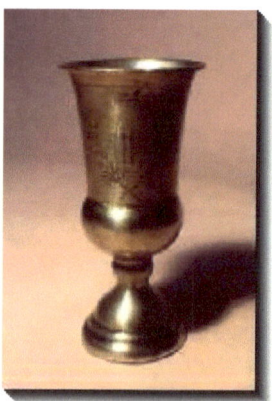
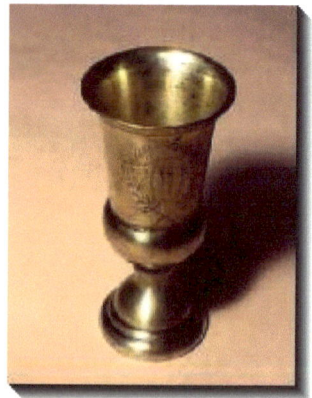
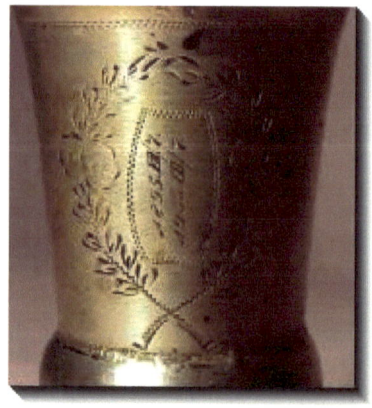

The visit to the Nyíregyháza Synagogue in Hungary was quite painful when I discovered that most of the Jewish ritual items were missing.

The young Rabbi took me to the nearby blacksmith. I was stunned to see a large collection of Judaica items on the shelves. The prices the blacksmith asked for the sale of some of the items were completely unreasonable.

When I asked him in Hungarian how he had accumulated such an impressive collection, the answer was, "I bought them during the war from a Rabbi as he had no money to buy food…"

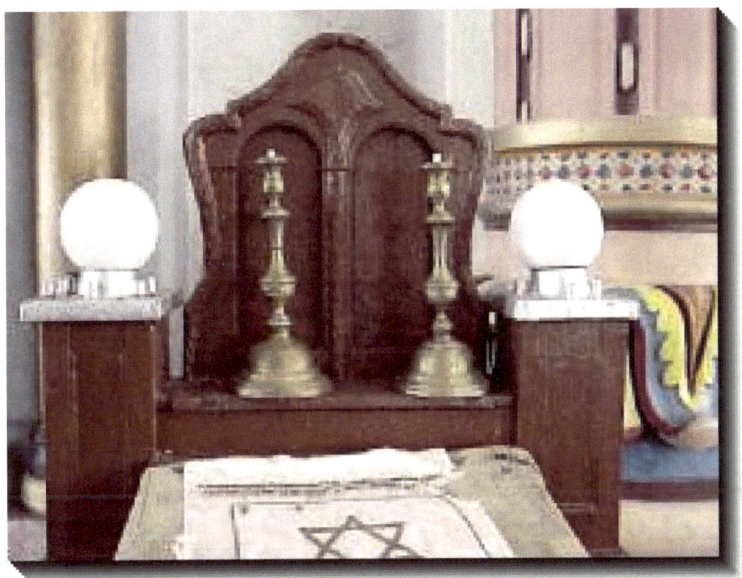

On the way back to Budapest, I stopped at a local Gypsy flea market. Among the wares of one of the merchants, spread on the ground, I found a pair of Tefillin (Phylacteries).

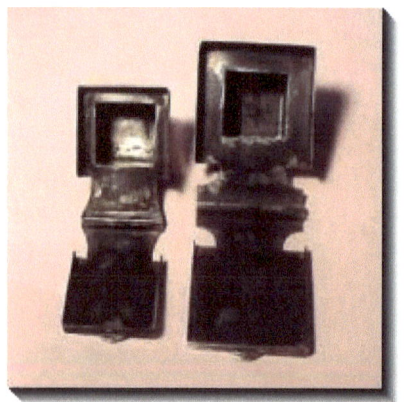

I tried very hard to hide my excitement when I bought them from the Gypsy dealer.

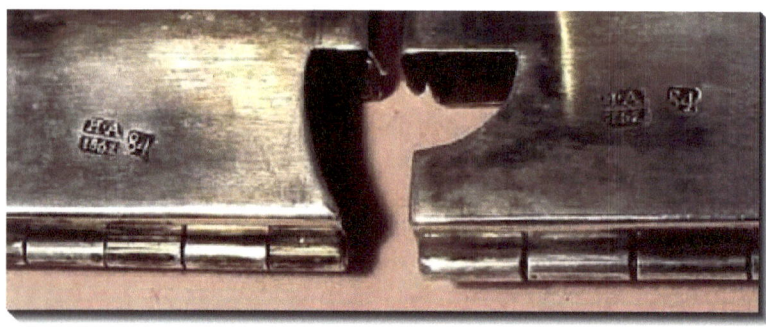

The Tefillin were covered by very rare 1861 Imperial Russian Silver covers…

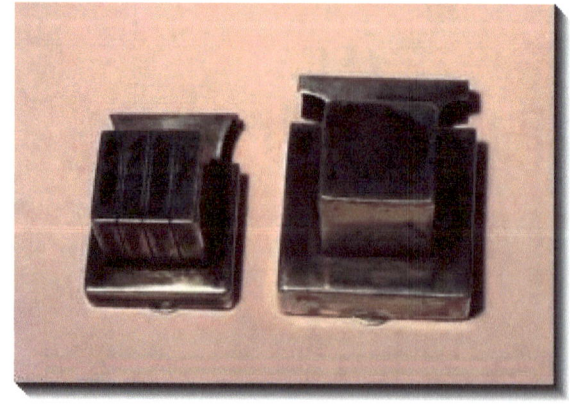

Another touching event was when I found a box in a small antique shop. The box, which was wrapped in a cloth, had belonged to a Cohen who had lost his entire family in the Holocaust.

The box contained, among other things, a book of Vayikra (Leviticus) dated 1887 with a silver cover. Inside on the first page there was a list of names and their WWII tattoo numbers…

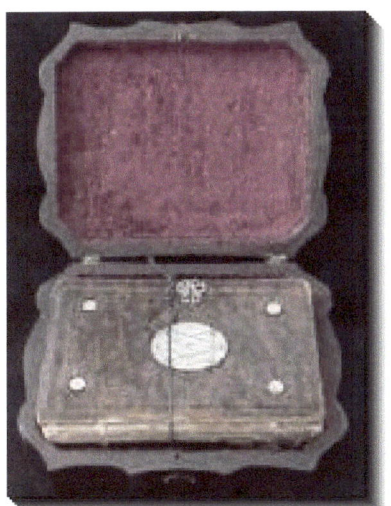
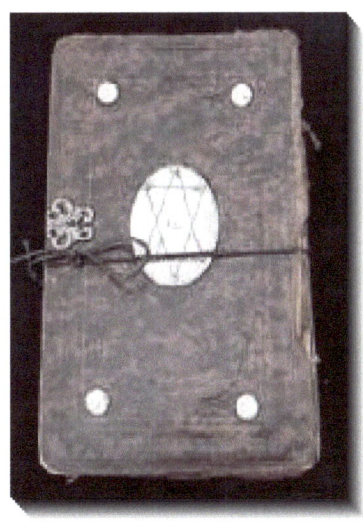
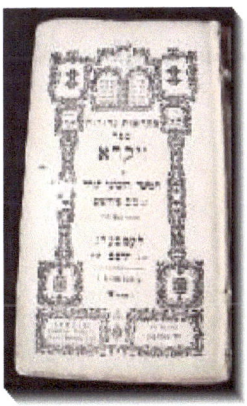
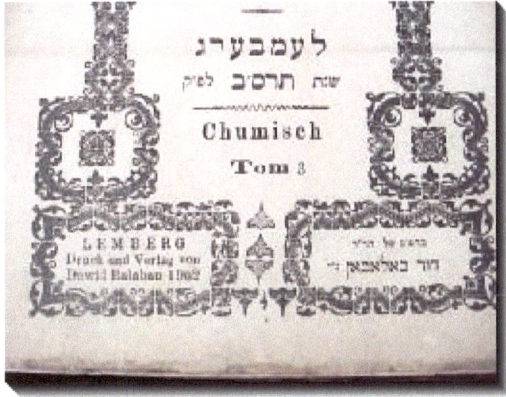

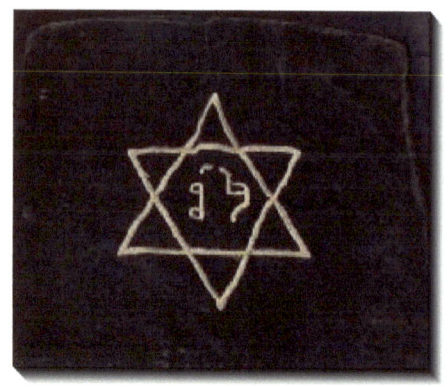
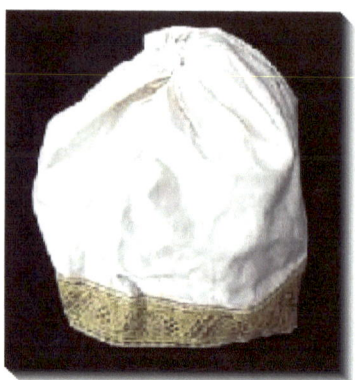
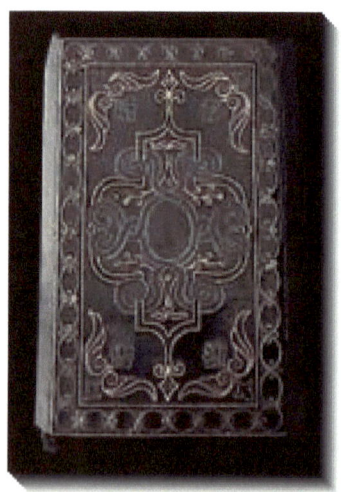
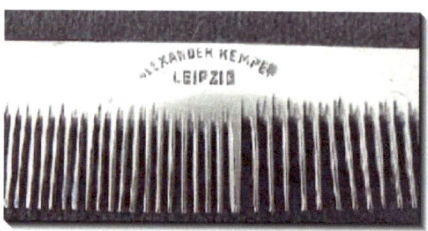
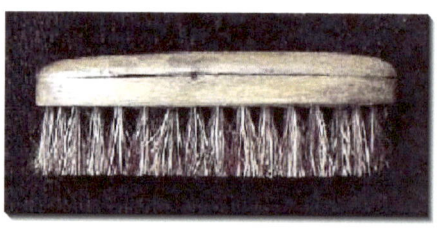
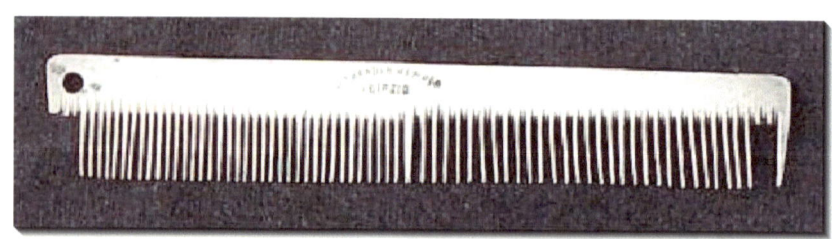

5. The Great Discovery in India

The Synagogue in Pune called *Ohel David* (Tent of David) was built in 1863 by David Sassoon. This Synagogue is built of red bricks, therefore it is called by the locals as the *Lal Davel* and it is one of the major Monuments of Pune.

Not far from the Synagogue, the Juna Bazaar flea-market is located. Beautiful copper artefacts that look like the remnants of ancient times are available at a low cost. Some of these pieces are true antiques and often date back to the medieval period.

There I found my copper cup.

It took me a while to realize that I could see Hebrew writing. After a short negotiation, I bought it. After thorough research, I can report that I had found one of the rarest and unique original authentic 19C Judaica items. It is a solid copper cup, with the engraving and inscription as seen below.

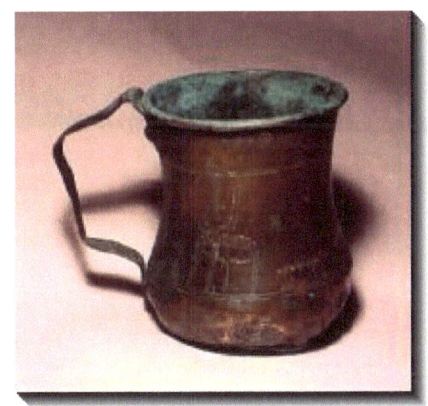

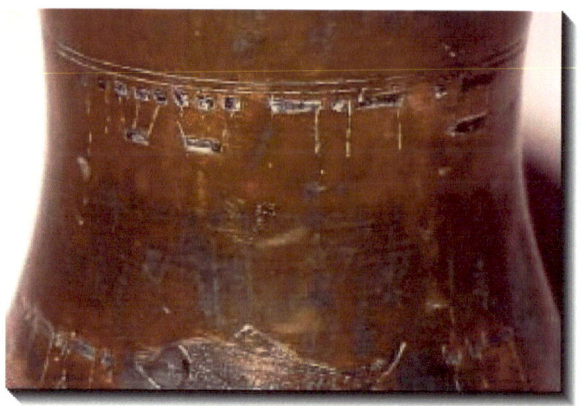

The cup has the name Sir David Sassoon engraved in old Hebrew characters; 'si' (senor or mister) David Sassoon. Below 'Dagan & Tirosh' (corn or grain, new wine), you may see a fish and a chair, which are status symbols.

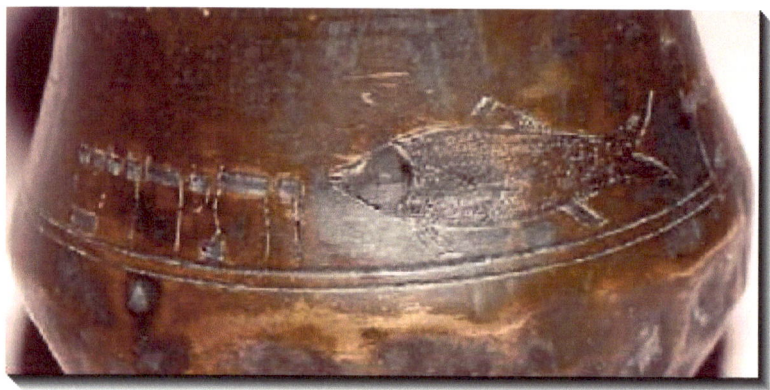

It was used for 'Mayim Achronim', 'Netilat Yadayim', or used for 'Zedaka' (charity) probably at *Ohel David* or possibly at *Bnei Israel* Synagogue in India. It has one handle typically used by Sefaradi-Iraqis. The two handles cups were mostly used by Ashkenazi Jews.

6. From Russia With Love

Most of my Russian collection has been acquired via auctions and from Russian immigrants to Israel since the 1980s. A few items I bought in Moscow in 1985. I heard exciting individual stories from the immigrants, about how they smuggled their items through Russian customs, while taking unnecessary risks. I must admit that I was quite generous with my price offering, trying to combine the item's value with my personal emotional value.

I was fascinated by the workmanship of the colour enamelled silver items, the delicate engraving in the silver ware, and the uniqueness of the Imperial Russian antiques.

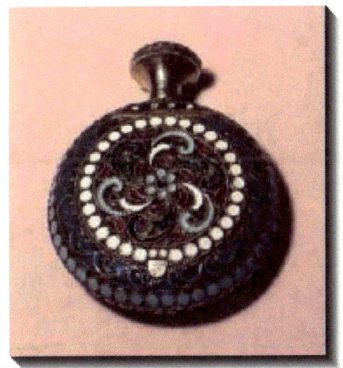 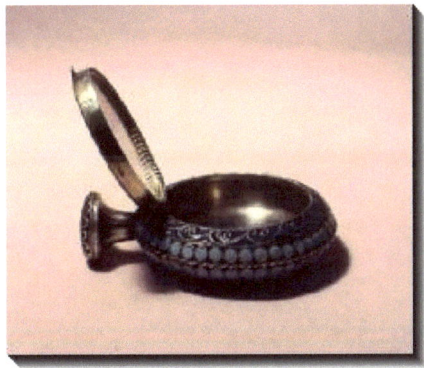

A rare Russian silver (916=88) and enamel perfume and compact, a unique combination (1908-1917).

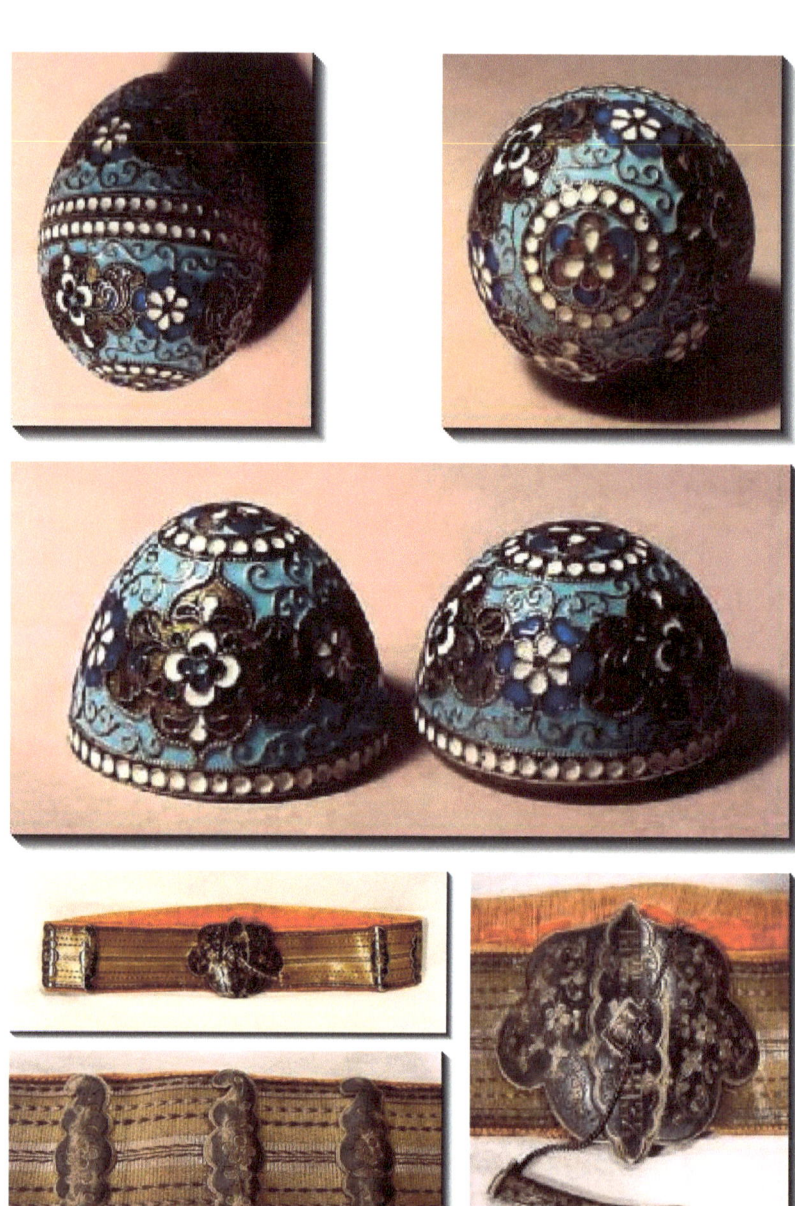

A rare Russian 19C silver (84) and niello Cossack
Caucasus original belt, with 7 niello silver ornaments.

A large gorgeous 19C Russian silver (84) open salt dish, superb quality Made in by Alexander Sevyer Moscow, 1892.

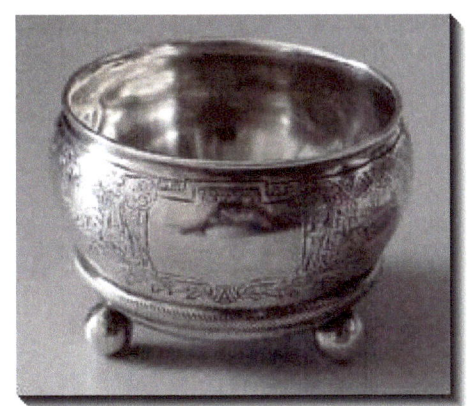

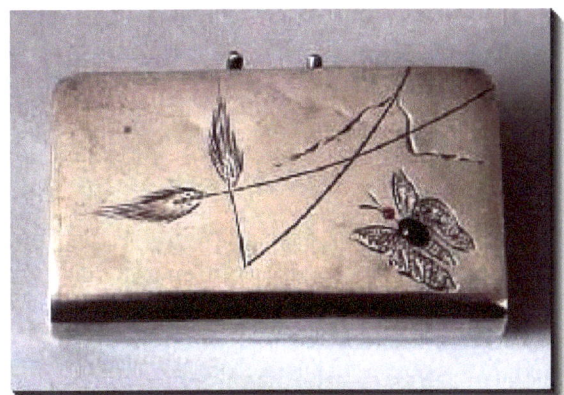

A Russian 19C art nouveau silver (84) and leather purse with inlaid **rubies**.

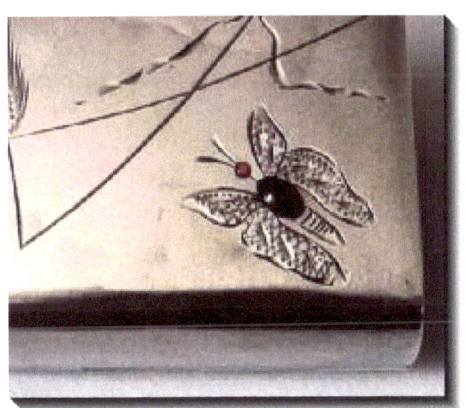

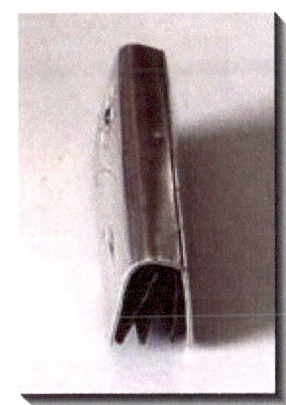

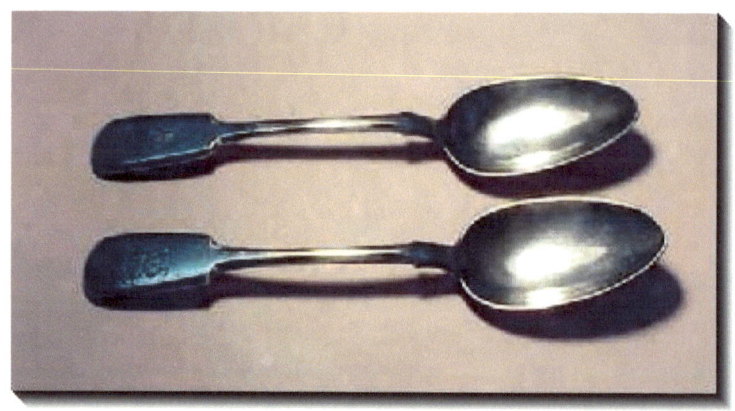

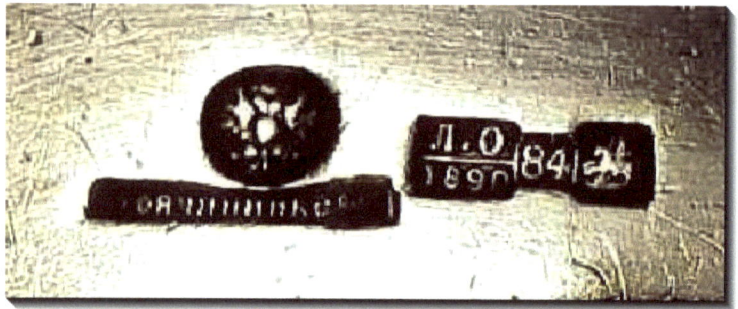

A rare pair of large and heavy Russian silver (84) spoons.
Made by the famous Russian silversmith P. Ovchinnikov in 1890.

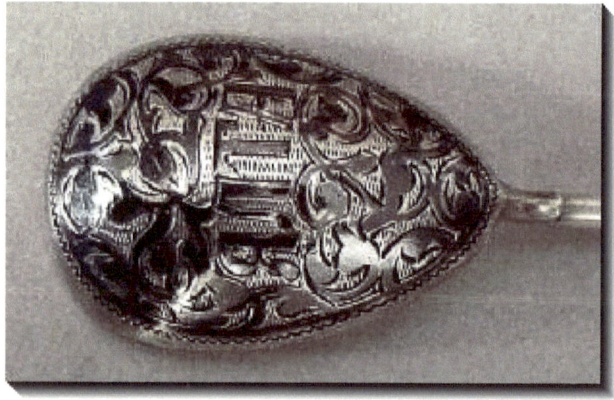

Gorgeous Russian silver (84) and niello, 19C spoon – Yalta.

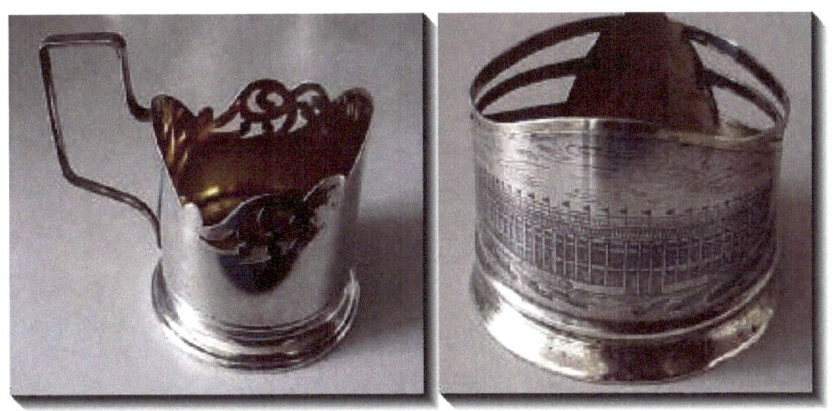

Imperial Russian tea-glass silver holders.

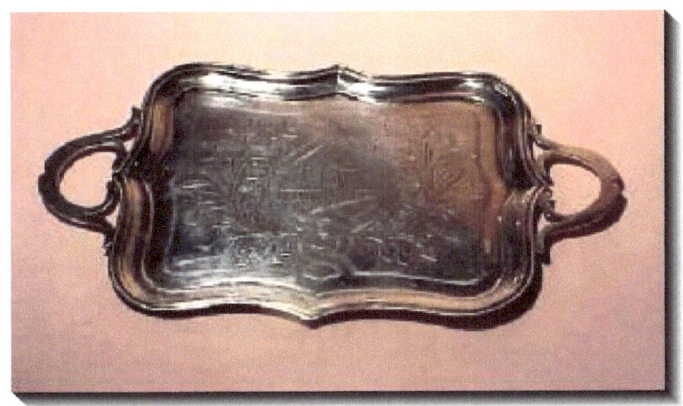

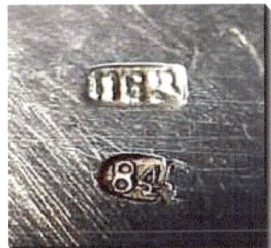
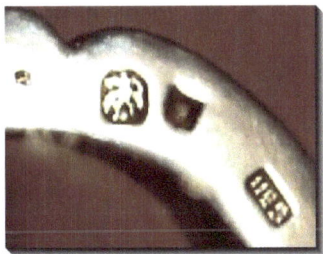

Imperial Russian 19C silver (84) serving tray.

7. Auctions and Fairs in England

While studying towards my Ph.D. in Medical Physics at the Royal Postgraduate Medical School, Hammersmith, London, during the late 1970s, I could not ignore the actions of the antique auctions and fairs in England.

Whenever I had the spare time and opportunity, I eagerly attended the many events and tried to buy interesting and unique items with my limited resources. I had the philosophy that it is desirable to purchase one *good* item, rather than spread the same budget over several lower quality items. It is easy to say so, but more difficult to implement it.

The following items are a sample of the large selection of antiques acquired via auctions and fairs.

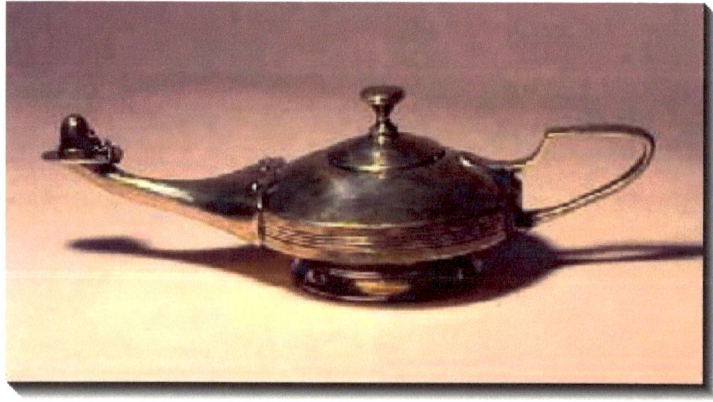

An Edwardian sterling silver Genies lamp, design lighter, Birmingham 1922.

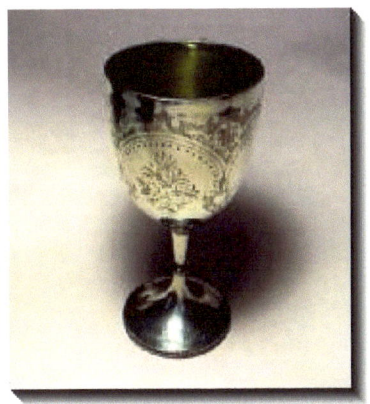 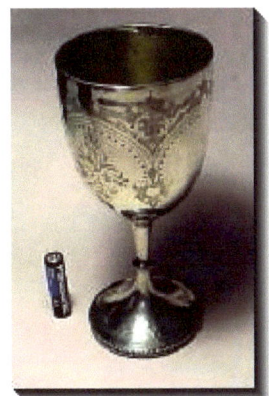

A gorgeous and rare sterling silver English goblet/chalice.
Made by the famous London silversmith Robert Hennell, 1870

Originally it was presented to the winner (A.F.W. Forhes)
of the quarter of a mile race in 1870.
Height: 7.6" (19.3 cm) ;Weight: 220 gram (7.8 oz)

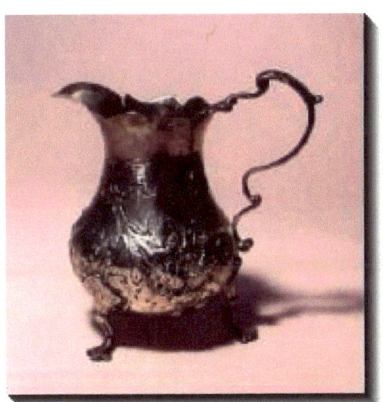 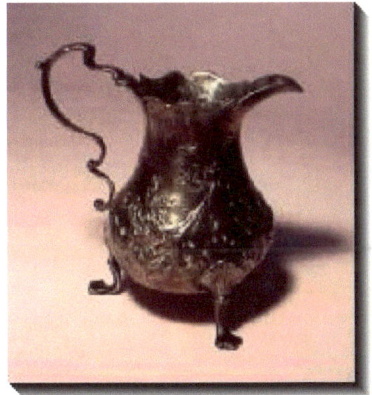

A George III sterling silver cream jug of pear-shape
on three scroll pad feet, the body chased with flowers and
foliage and applied with a double scroll handle,
London 1763
Height: 3 1/2" (9 cm).

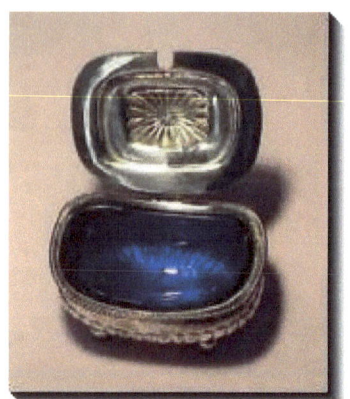
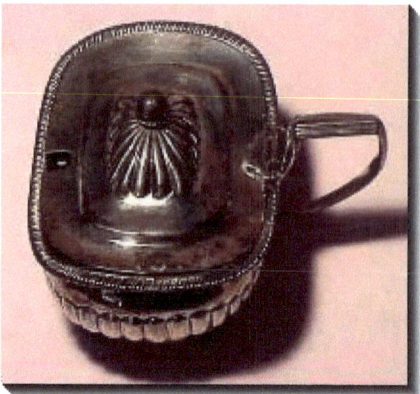
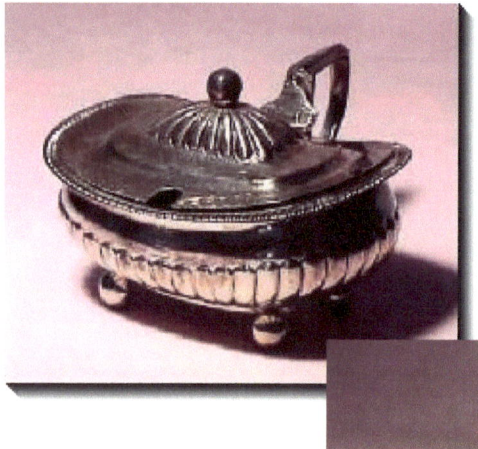

A Regency sterling silver mustard pot of part-fluted molded oblong form,
on ball feet and with a blue glass liner, gadrooned border,
bracket handle and part-fluted domed hinged cover with ball finial,
the front engraved with a crest, Solomon Royes & John East Dix,
London 1818 - 3 1/2" (9cm).

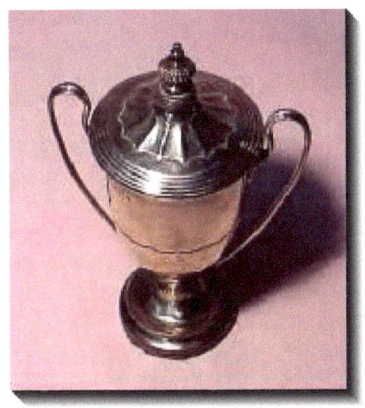 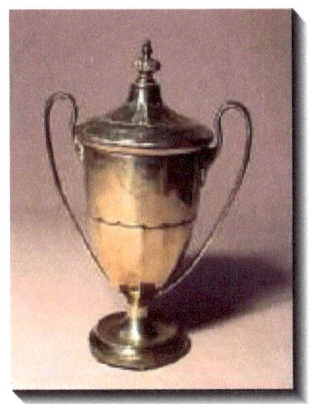

A sterling silver trophy with cover, Birmingham 1928

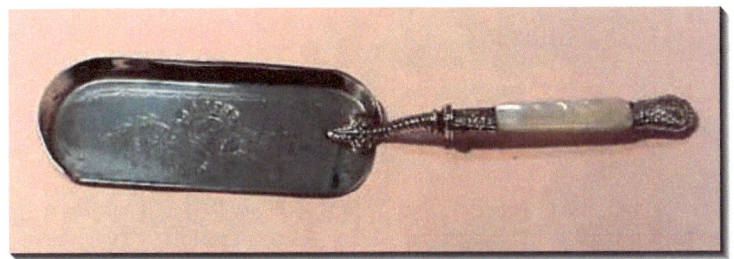

A gorgeous English crumber made by Mappin & Webb,
Princess plate with mother of pearl handles.

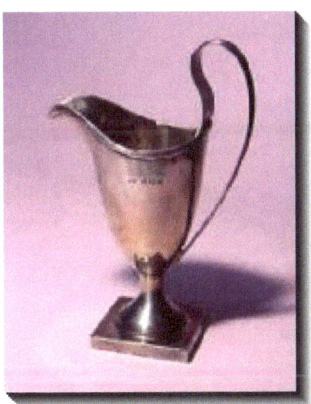

A sterling silver cream jug, on square shaped feet,
Birmingham, England 1907.

8. Judaica

The terminology of Judaica refers mainly to Jewish ceremonial art, including a list of objects used by Jews for ritual purposes.

There are Jewish Museums worldwide containing rare and unique Judaica ceremonial collections. In addition to Israel, there are Jewish museums in the U.S., such as in New York and in San Francisco, and in Europe we have such museums in London, Paris, Prague and elsewhere around the world.

A specific selection of Judaica items are displayed here.

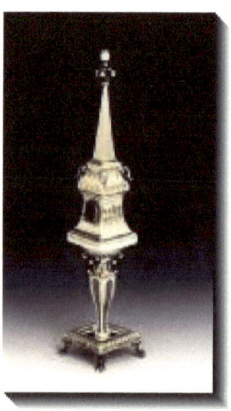 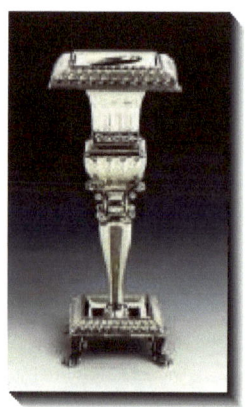

Part of the Havdalah ceremony, following the close of Shabbat, is by sniffing a spice within the spice box or the spice tower and lighting a candle in the Havdalah candle holder.

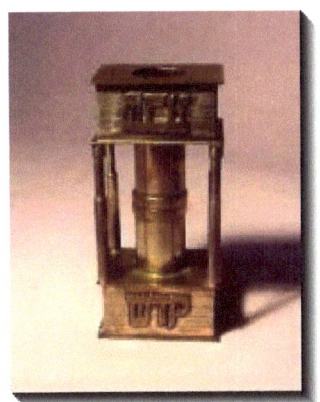
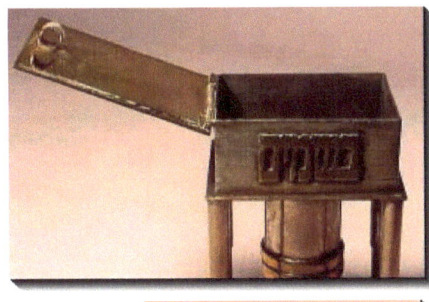
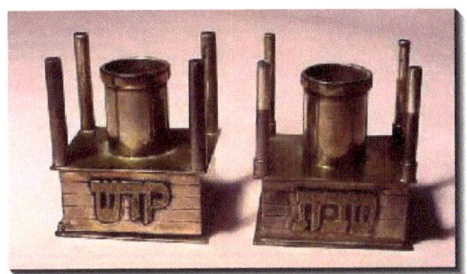
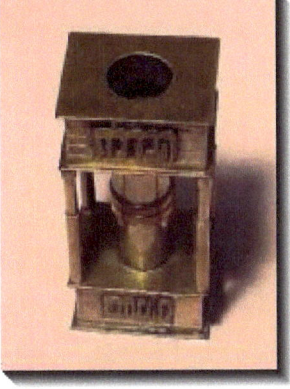

This is a unique Judaica artwork for multiple religious usages.
It is a spice box, a candle holder for Havdalah and Shabbat candleholders.
The words of "Shabbat, Kodesh, Havdalah, Besamim" are in brass.
It is made of sterling silver and brass by the artist Gabi Mamazav
Only 250 were made, this is 82/250.

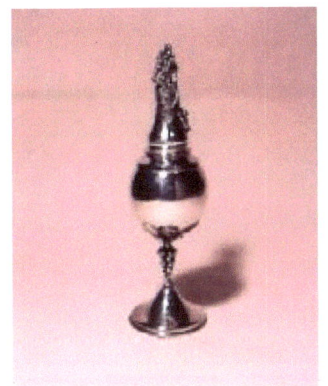
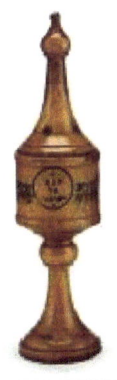
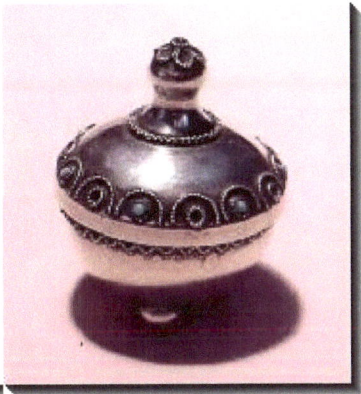

Silver, olive wood and filigree spice boxes.

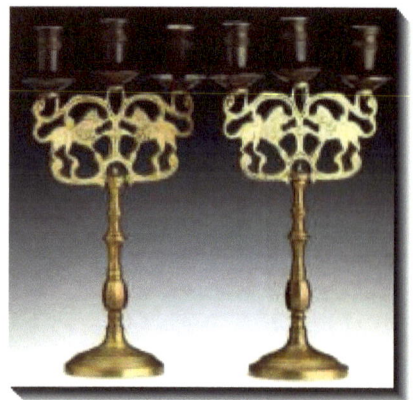

A pair of early 20C brass Sabbath candlesticks, made in the US according to the 17C original made in Poland

A pair of rare huge Russian made 19C brass candlesticks.

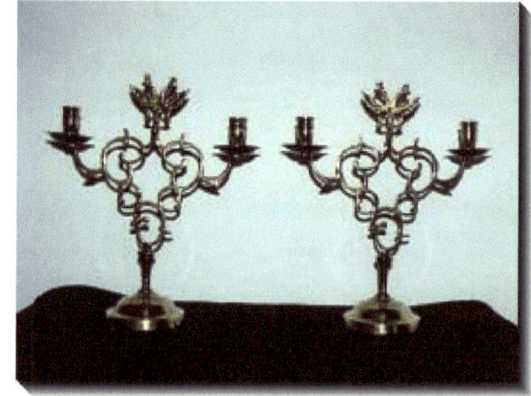

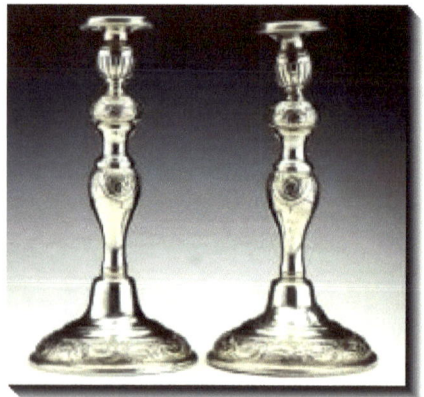

A pair of sterling silver hand chased early 20C Sabbath candlesticks made according to Polish design of 19C.

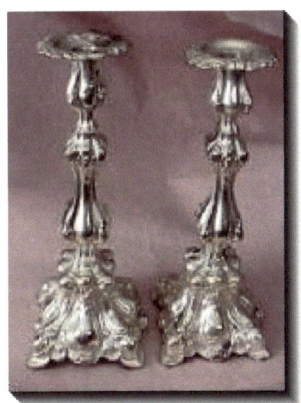
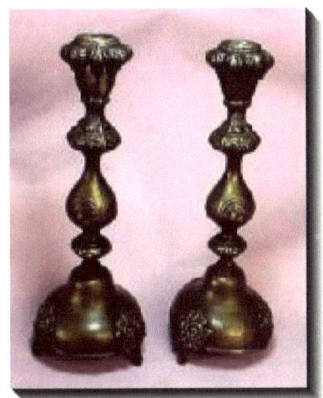

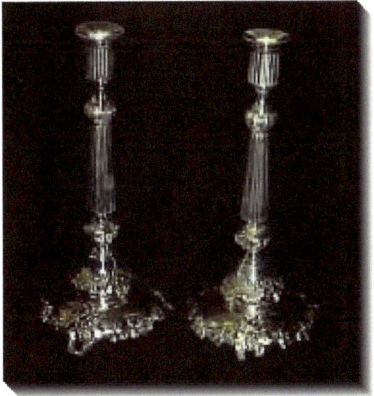

Sabbath 19C Polish candlestics.

Early Israeli olive wood Sabbath candlesticks made in 1950s by Bezalel.

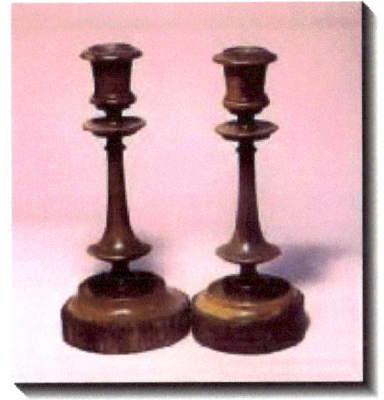

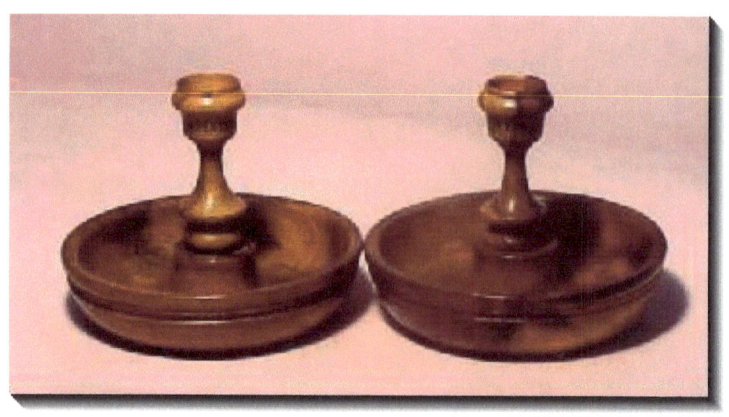

A pair of candlesticks made of olive wood, Israel 1950s.
Used mainly for travel, they are folding.

The Newark International Antiques and Collectors Fair is the largest event of its kind in Europe. It is held at the Newark and Nottinghamshire eighty-four acre showground, with up to 2,500 stands. Thousands of dealers and buyers attend from around the world.

I have found many unique items there during my visits to England. I have a visual memory; accordingly, I was walking quite quickly, passing the stands. I am not so keen about brass items, especially the new ones. I passed a stand with only brass items on the table, all carefully shined by the dealer, as most dealers in England would do.

Suddenly, I felt that I had seen something familiar, but I could not determine what. I went back to the stand and again observed the items on the table, but still, I could not tell what made me stop.

After passing through a few stands, suddenly it hit me. I went back and I saw a shiny pair of candlesticks.

According to the asking price, I realized that the dealer did not know the history and the real value of those candlesticks. After a short and 'light' negotiation, I bought them.

Those candlesticks were a rare pair of nineteen century brass Sabbath candlesticks, made by the renowned Polish maker Jakubowski & Jarra. It seems that they were extensively cleaned by the dealer. I found the maker's signature engraved on the bottom rim of the candlesticks. The reason that I had apparently stopped was because I was reminded by their shape that I had seen a similar pair at the synagogue in Budapest (p. 25).

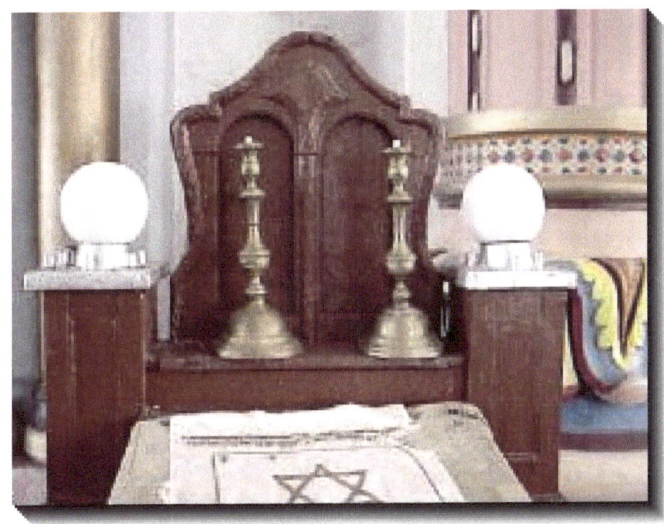

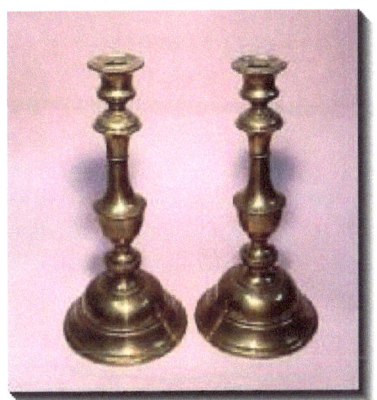

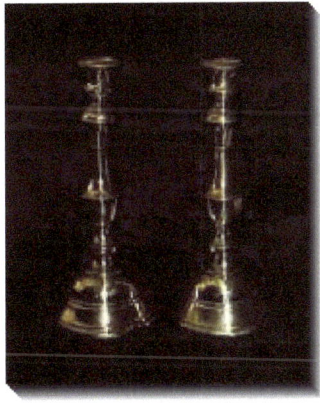

A rare 19C Polish brass Sabbath candlesticks, made by the renowned Polish maker Jakubowski & Jarra, with original rich golden patina.

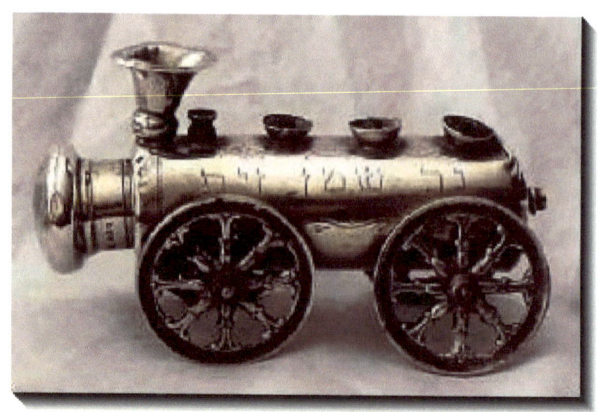

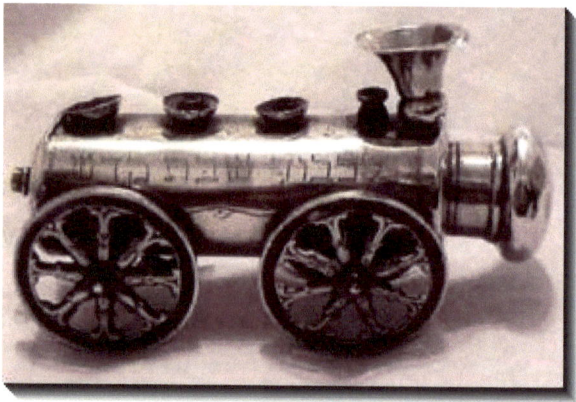

A locomotive shape unique and rare silver Sabbath oil candle.
It was made in 1909 in England from sterling silver perfume bottle.
Hebrew inscriptions: "Ner Shemen Zayit" ('Olive oil candle') and
"Lichvod Shabat Kodesh" ('In honor of the Holy Sabbath').

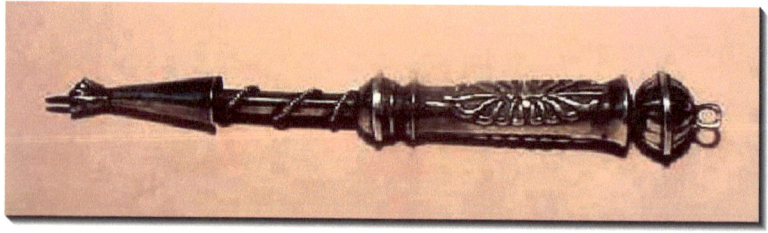

A Rare Russian 19C silver (84) Torah pointer.

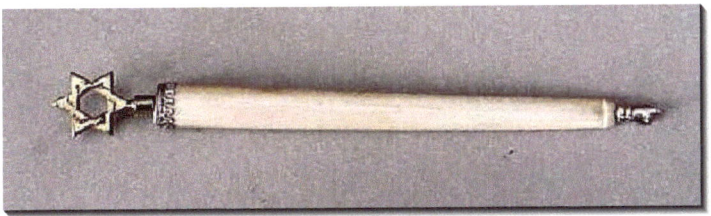

A sterling silver and ivory Torah Pointer.

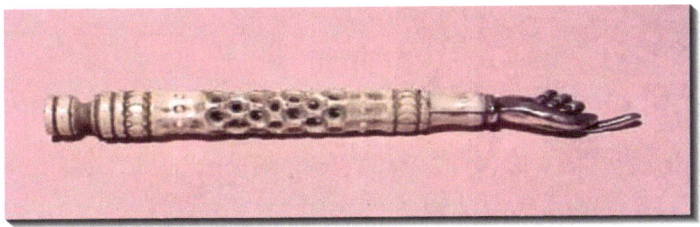

A sterling silver Torah Pointer mounted on a bone hollow handle with spice compartment.

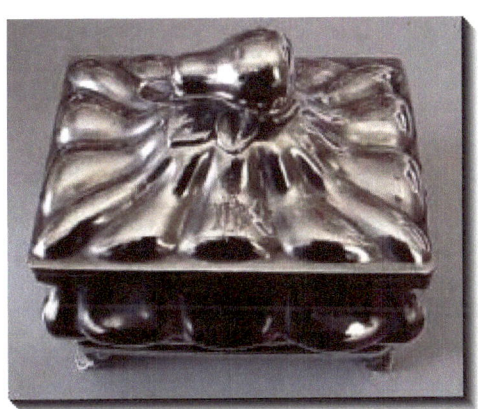

A gorgeous 19C silver Polish large Etrog box.

Etrog (Esrog) refers to the yellow citron or citrus used by Jews on the week-long holiday of Sukkot. The Etrog is protected by silky flax fiber and stored in a box usually made of silver.

And you shall take on the 1st day the fruit of beautiful trees, branches of palm trees and boughs of leafy trees and willows of the brook, and you shall rejoice before the Lord your God 7 days! (Leviticus 23:40).

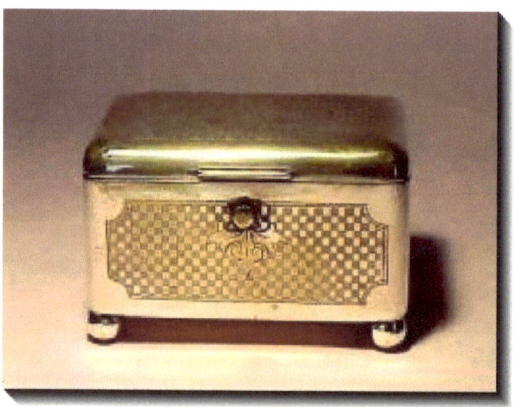

A silver plated Etrog/Esrog box made in Poland by Norblin, early 20C.

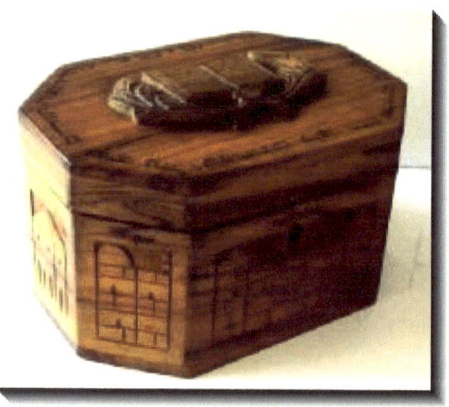

A rare olive wood Etrog box made in Jerusalem, early 20C
(Sotheby's sale - Bezalel and Israeliana - Tel-Aviv
May 11, 1998, page 79 lot # 242, est.$ 800-$ 1200)

Kiddush is a blessing recited over wine or grape juice to sanctify the Shabbat and Jewish holidays. Traditionally Kiddush cups, beakers and goblets are made of silver and are highly collectable.

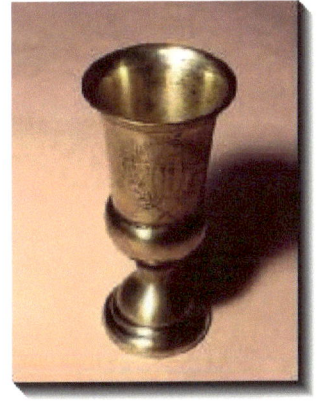
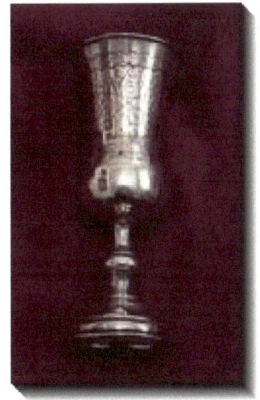
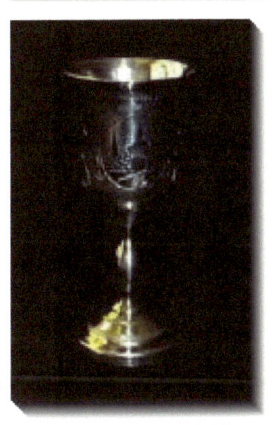
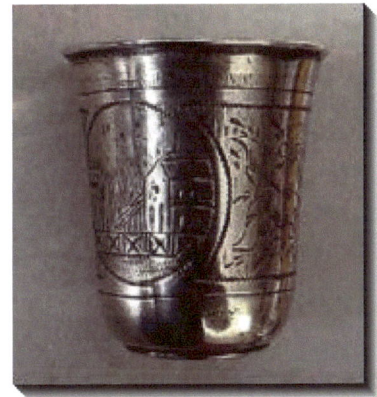
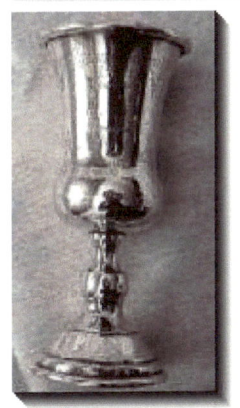
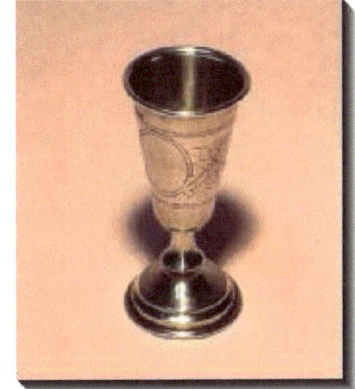

Hanukkah is an eight-day Jewish holiday commemorating the rededication of the Holy Temple in Jerusalem at the time of the Maccabean Revolt in the second century BCE. It is a festival of lights and is observed for eight days by the kindling of the lights of a unique candelabrum.

The typical Menorah/Hanukkah lamp consists of eight branches with an additional branch, called the *shamash* or attendant in Hebrew. The Hanukkah lamp is made of metal, usually silver, but also from other material, such as pottery, and it is highly collectable.

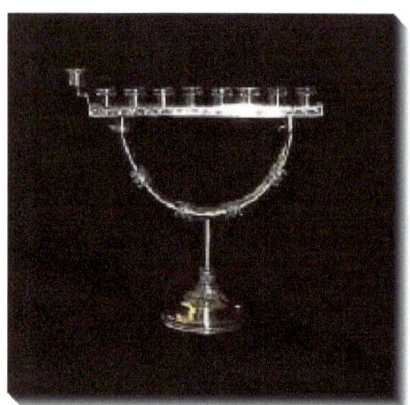 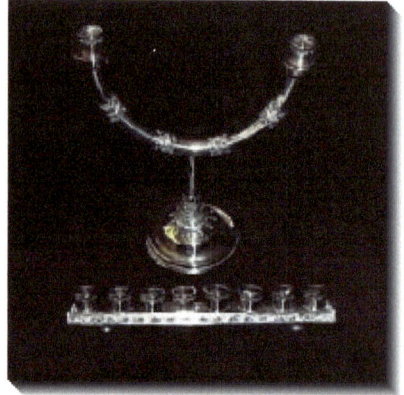

A sterling silver Hanukkah and Sabbath lamp, made about the 1950s by Bezalel, Jerusalem.

A beautiful Hanukkah lamp, made by Pal-Bell during the 1950s. It is made of lacquered and enamelled-verdigris brass and highly sought after by collectors.

Pal-Bell was founded In Israel in 1939 by Maurice Ascalon (known as Moshe Klein).

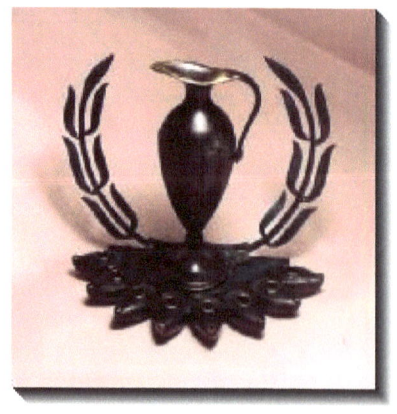

9. Made in Palestine and Israel

In this chapter, Israeli made items are displayed; a few items were made during the Palestine era pre 1948. These items are highly collectable and they are quite difficult to find.

Pal-Bell made items are highly collectable; one of the top items is the Hanukkah lamp described earlier.

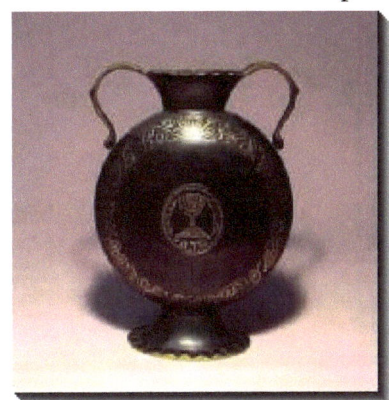
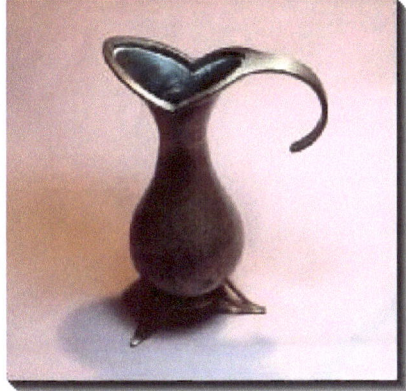
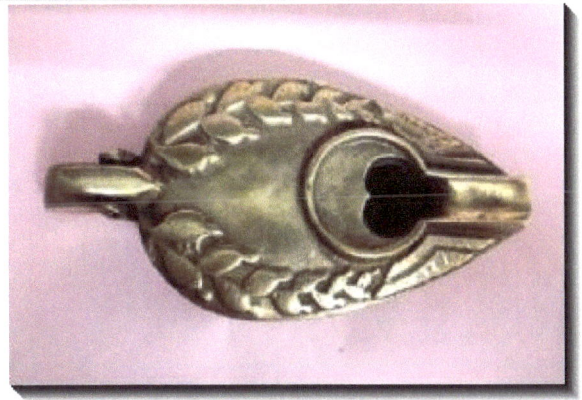

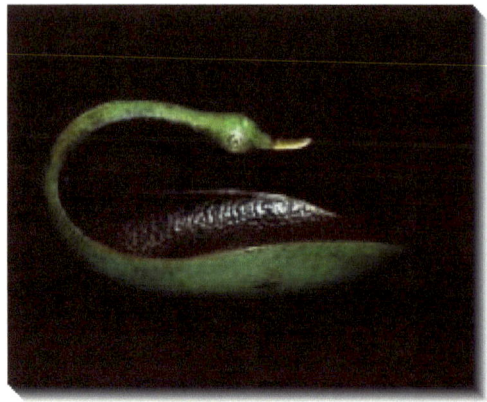
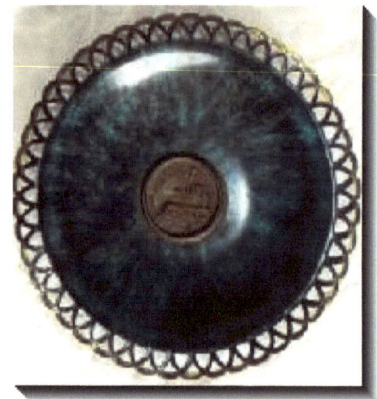
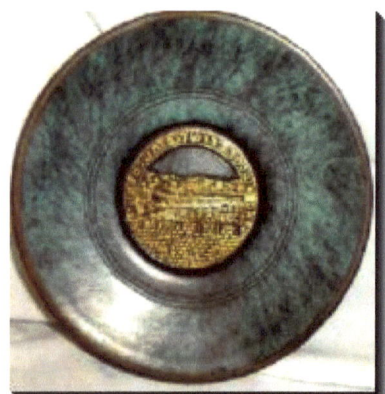
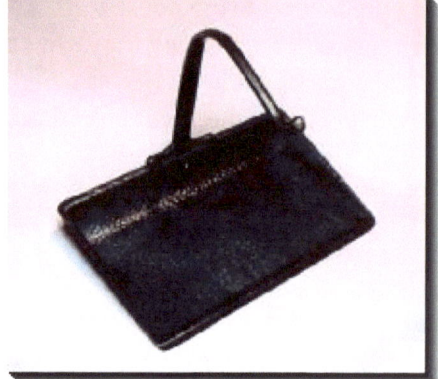

Hans Teppich was born in Germany in 1904. After finishing High-School in Berlin, he learned woodcarving and worked in a furniture factory for three years.

During this period, he studied art in evening classes, and then continued studying for ten more years in morning classes in the "Kunstgewerbe und Handwerkerschule" in Berlin. He acquired a broad range of art education, including: drawing, sculpture, metalwork, bronze casting, metal turning, and interior design.

Hans Teppich won many prizes during his studies for different projects in which he participated.

His bronze and stone sculptures of animals were presented at an exhibition at the Berlin Zoo.

In 1933, he emigrated to Israel and established a workshop in Jerusalem. In his workshop he created different practical art objects, including Hanukkah Lamps, Candlesticks, Mezuzot, Israeli flower-shaped Spice Boxes, together with many beautiful pieces of jewellery and unique chess sets.

Teppich was a genius artist. He became famous for his Biblical figures and Judaic items.

Hans Teppich passed away in 1983 at the age of 79 in Israel.

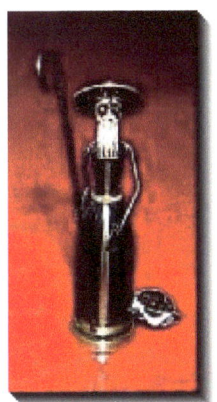
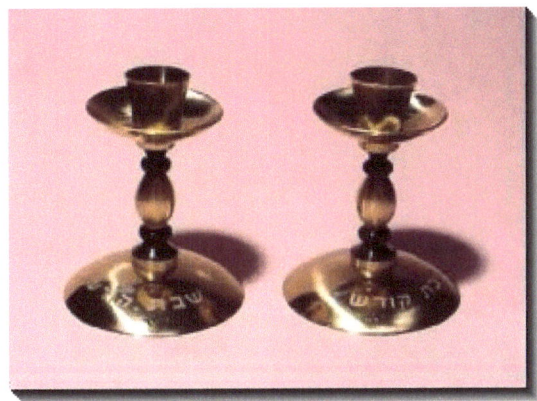
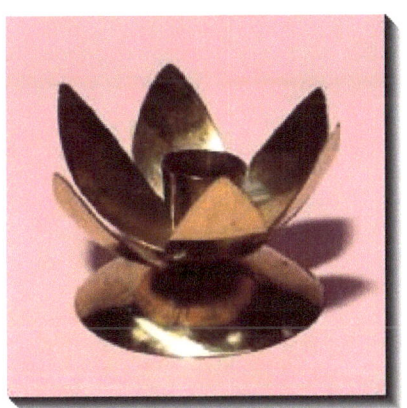
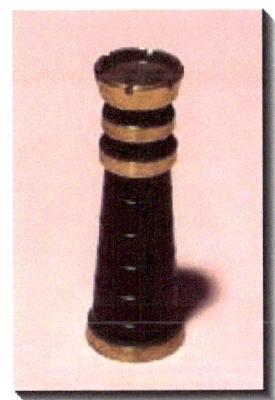

The displayed items in the metal ware category were made by various makers, currently not as well known as Pal-Bell or Oppenheim, but they are already very collectable and I predict that they will become more known in the future.

Some of those makers were employees at Pal-Bell, and after a few years of 'learning the business', they opened their own workshop. Oppenheim was already known prior to the 1950s and made items marked: "Hand Made in Palestine". Later they bought Pal-Bell from Moshe Klein and continued some product lines using Pal-Bell's moulds and their new logo.

During the transition period, we can see items marked with both logos and some have no marking at all, but the items were made by using the original Pal-Bell moulds. There are many original items made by Pal-Bell, not marked or not listed in the catalogues. Because certain items were made in a modular interchangeable manner, we may see certain 'marriages', which might be very successful; all of them, however, are highly collectable.

It was a very rich period, with designers such as Zeev Raban and others, together with new immigrants from Europe and Russia that contributed significantly to innovative and unique Israeli products.

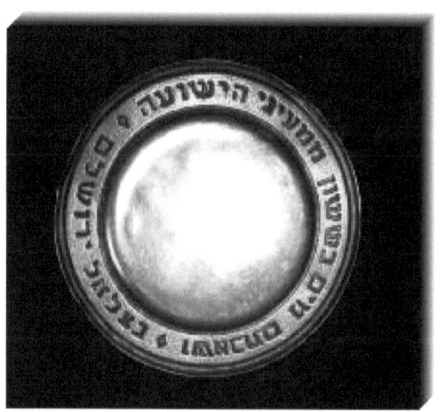

A sterling silver plate by Bezalel, Jerusalem.

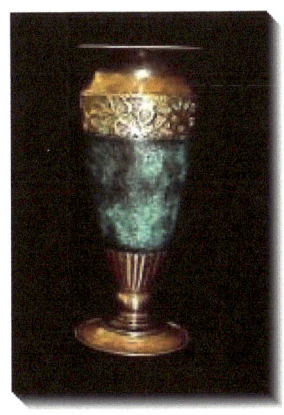
Oppenheim.

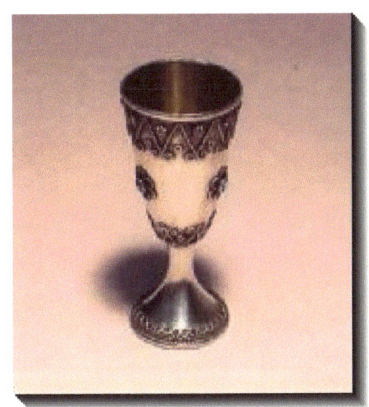
Stanetzky

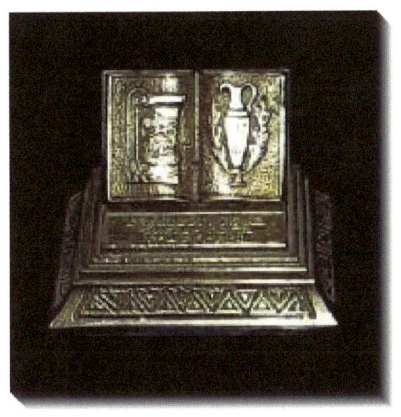
Israel Independence 1948.

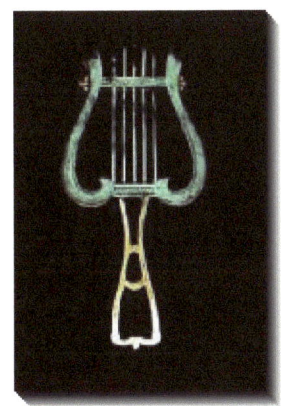
Tzel-Zion.

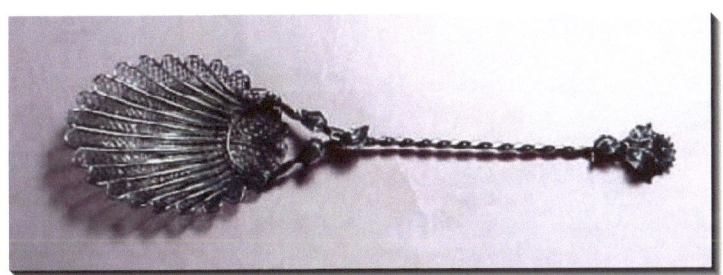
Silver filigree spoon, Bezalel.

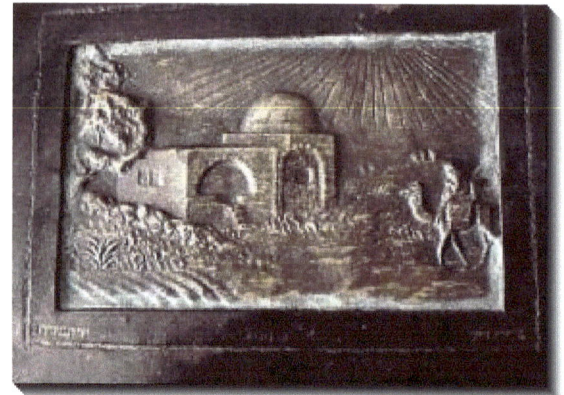

Rachel's tomb, an album by Bezalel.

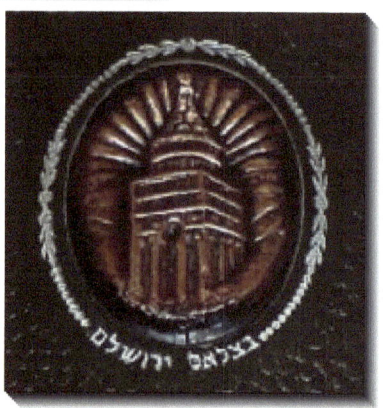

A rare bridge player's note book by Bezalel, Jerusalem.

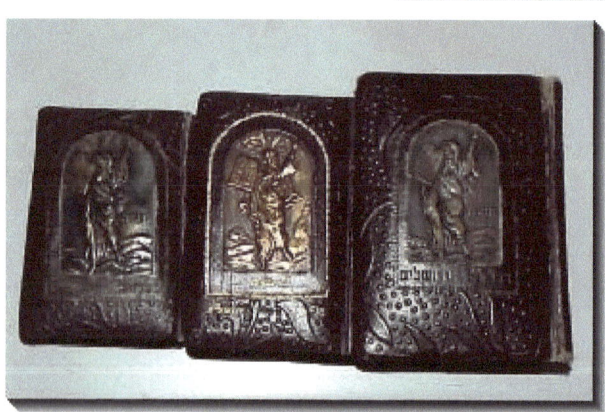

Bibles with a copper plaque depicting Moses with the Ten Commandments, Bezalel Jerusalem.

One of the segments in the Israeli Militaria collection is badges; among them, those of the Palestine era are highly collectable.

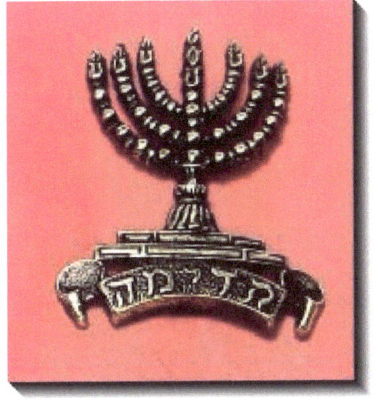

This Menorah shaped badge was used by the Jewish Legion, volunteers to the British Royal Fusiliers in Palestine, post World-War-I. It has the Hebrew word *Kadima* (forward) engraved upon it.

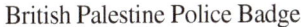
British Palestine Police Badge.

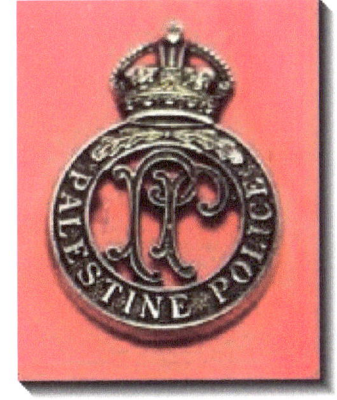

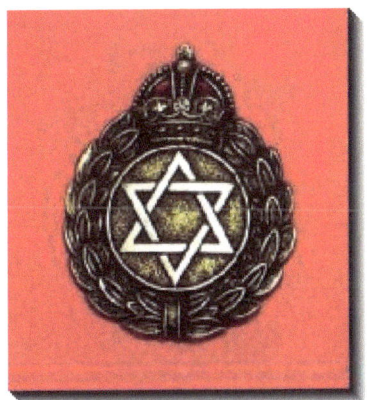
WWII British Army Jewish Chaplain Badge.

Yitzhak Rabin (1922–1995) was the fifth Prime Minister of Israel. He was a politician, statesman and general, who won the Nobel Peace Prize in 1994. Yitzhak Rabin was assassinated on November 4, 1995.

Bet Gabriel is located on the shores of the Sea of Galilee. It was established in 1993 by the Gabriel Sherover Foundation, and headed by the late Mrs. Gitta Sherover, in memory of her beloved son - Gabriel. She was a well known Israeli philanthropist who died on June 13, 2004.

In November 1994, a historical occasion took place in Bet Gabriel, when the peace treaty between Jordan and Israel was reconfirmed by the late King Hussein of Jordan and Israeli Prime Minister Yitzhak Rabin.

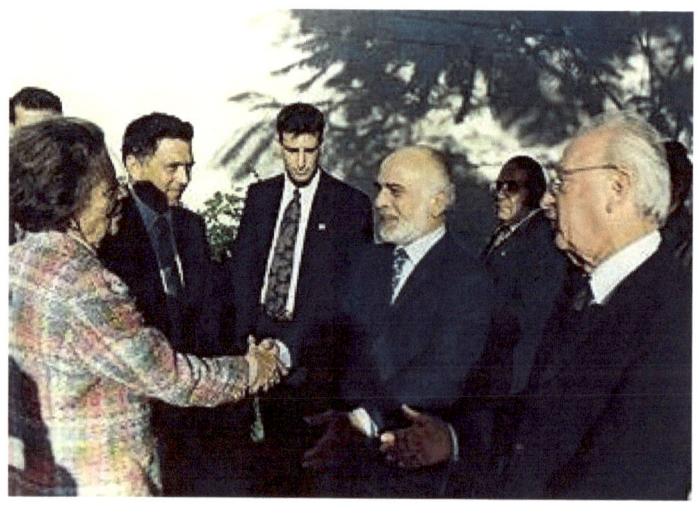

The following Islamic plate/charger, with silver inlaid damascene work, was given to Gitta Sherover by Yithak Rabin, the Prime Minister of Israel, on August 8, 1995, about three months before he was assassinated.

The plate has a plaque in Hebrew on its back: "To Gitta for your support, respectfully the Prime Minister", dated 8.8.95

Her estate was auctioned for the benefit of the Gabriel Sherover foundation and I bought this unique plate.

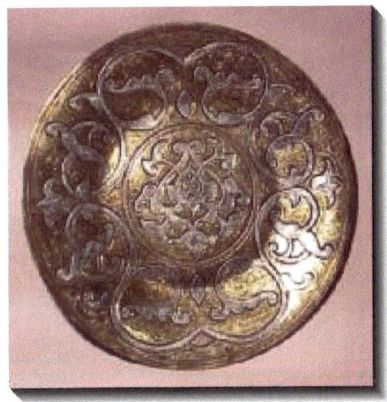

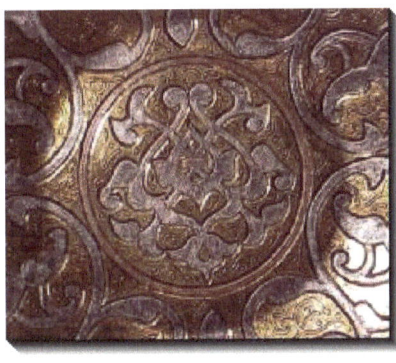

Diameter: 13.5" (16.5 cm);
Weight: 1,249 gram (44 oz)

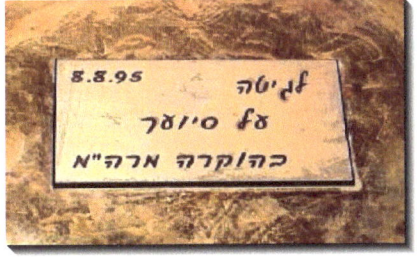

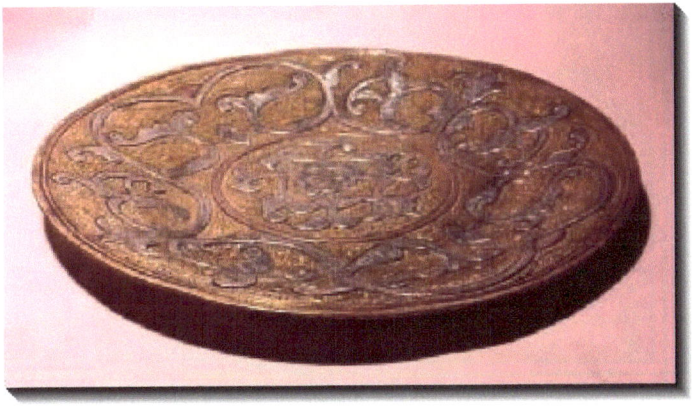

10. Wooden Made Items

Most items presented here were made of olive wood in Israel around the 1950s and some earlier during Palestine era. Items marked "Yerushalem" in Hebrew (without the letter 'yod') are highly collectable. Certain items were made by Bezalel are also highly collectable.

When collecting wooden ware, especially made of olivewood, we have to accept certain age related small splits or blemishes, which are typical to natural olive wood. Hand made pairs, such vases or candlesticks are never 100% identical.

I love wood, especially olive wood with age-related rich and dark patina. Here are few items from my collection.

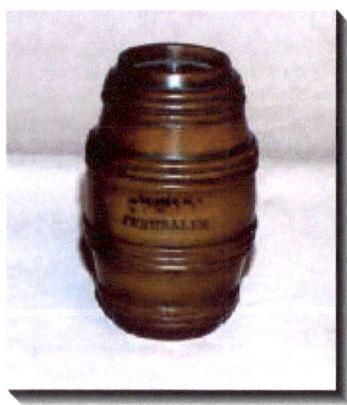 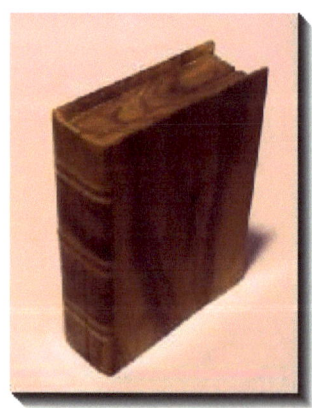

A barrel made of olive wood, marked Jerusalem, Palestine.

A box in the shape of a book made of olive wood, Jerusalem Palestine.

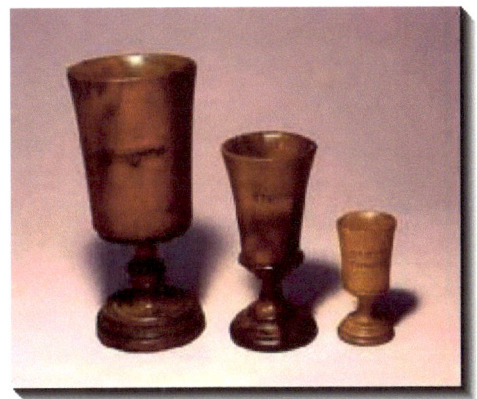

Rare Kiddush goblets made of olive wood, Israel 1900.

A pair of vases made of olive wood by Bezalel, Israel 1950s.

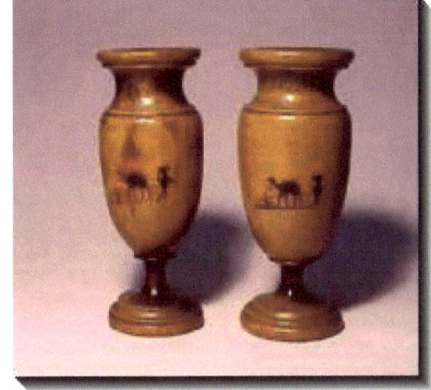

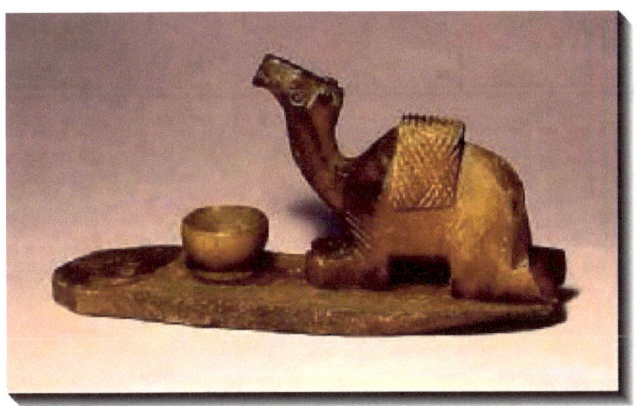

A resting camel made of olive wood, Israel, 1950-s

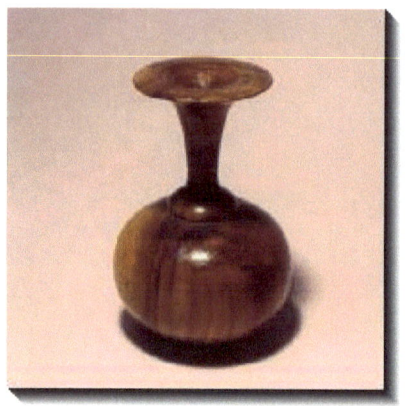

A rare shape of vase, made of olive wood.

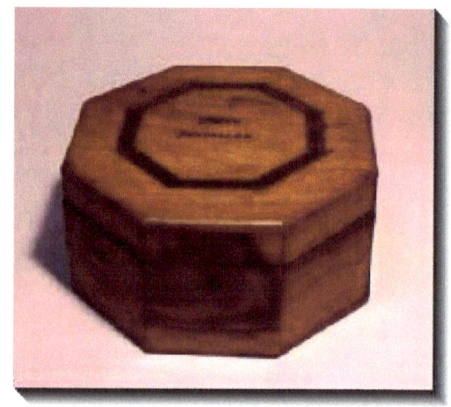

A very rare huge box made of olive wood, Jerusalem **Palestine** era.

H: 3.5" (9 cm) ; L: 7.1" (18 cm)
W: 7.1" (18 cm)

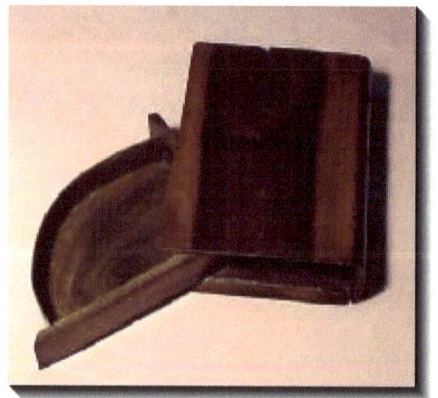

A very rare box in the shape of a book, made of olive wood, Jerusalem **Palestine** era.

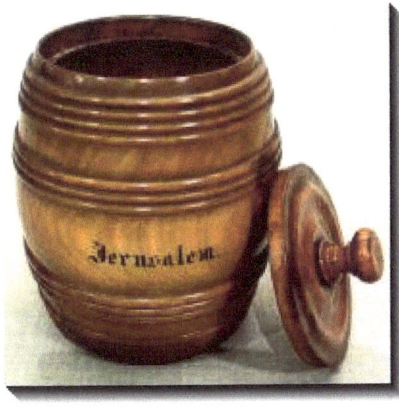
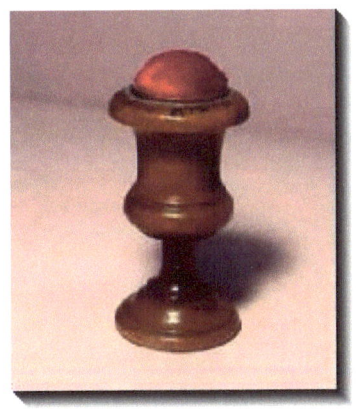

A rare barrel shape container made of olive wood, Jerusalem Palestine.

A pin cushion, made of olive wood Jerusalem Palestine.

A rare jewelry box made of olive wood, Bezalel Jerusalem Palestine.

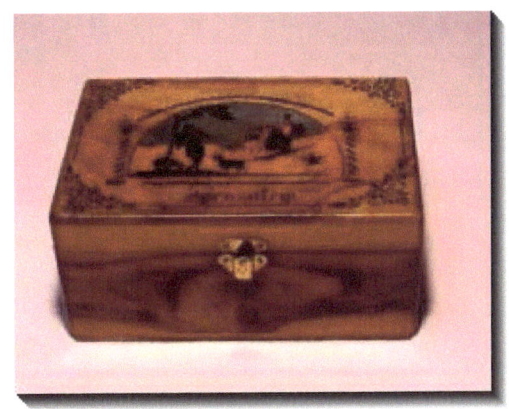

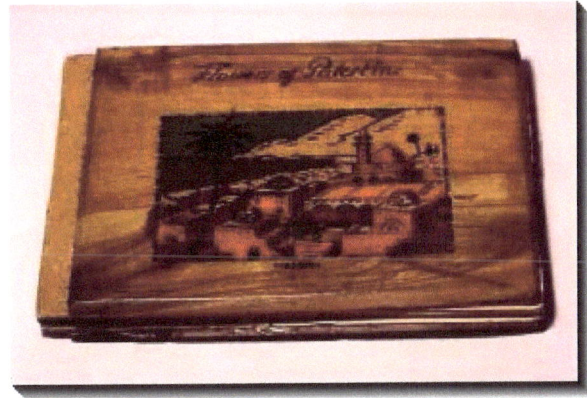

An olive wood covered pictures and flowers album, Tiberias, Palestine.

Original letter by Otto Koenig from Bible House, New York from April 11th 1914.

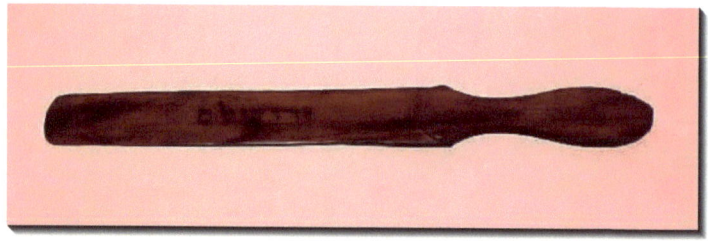

A letter opener/page turner made in Palestine, marked Jerusalem.

A napkin ring made of olive wood, Palestine era.

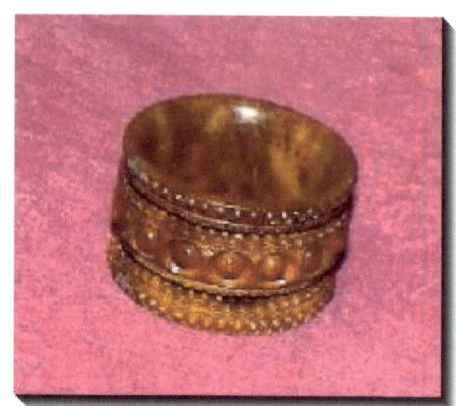

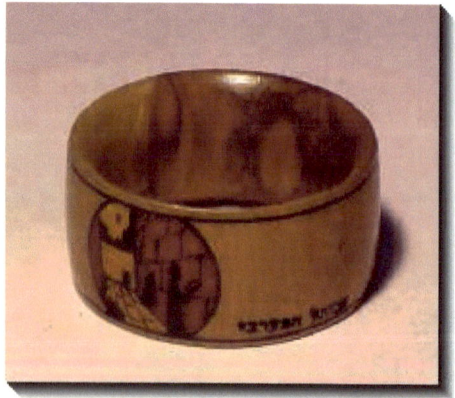

A rare olive wood napkin ring made by Bezalel, The Wailing Wall.

Sorrento is a small town in Campania, southern Italy. Since the early 19th Century, Sorrento has been known for its unique inlayed and marquetry work. One of the typical marks is the swallow. A unique and rare collection is displayed here.

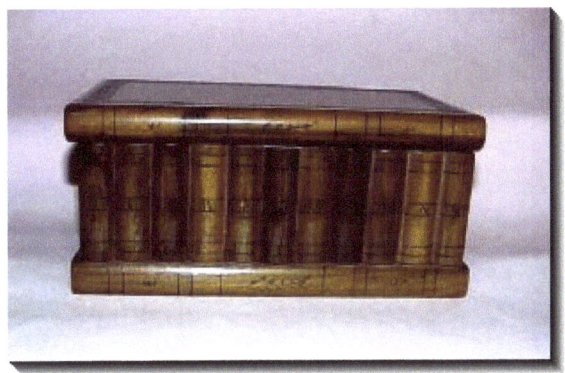

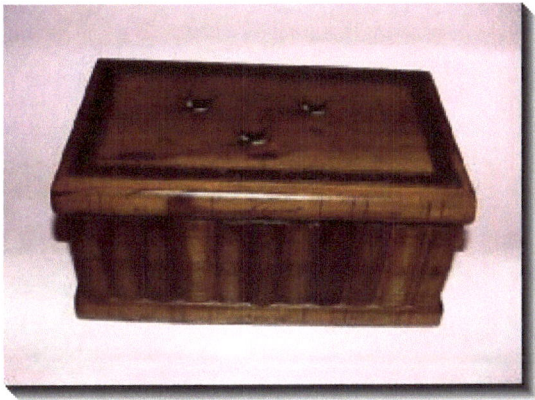

A gorgeous and rare late 19C Sorrento puzzle box.

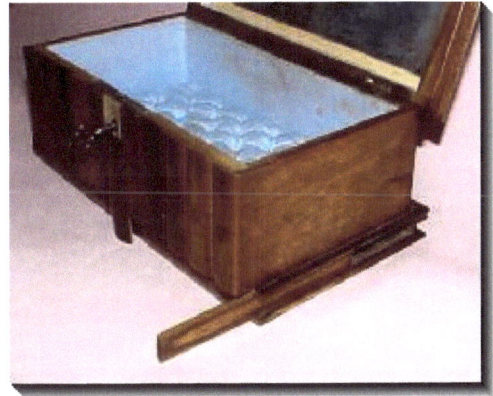

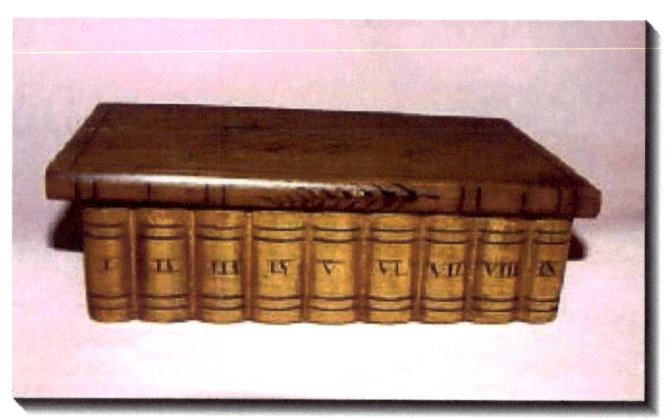

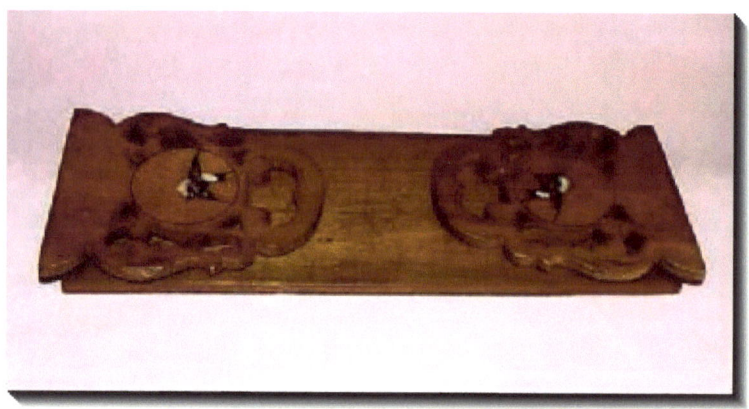

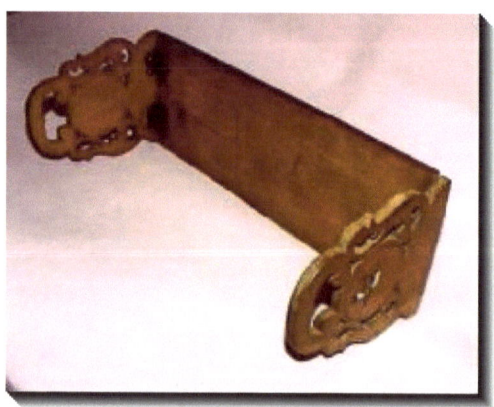

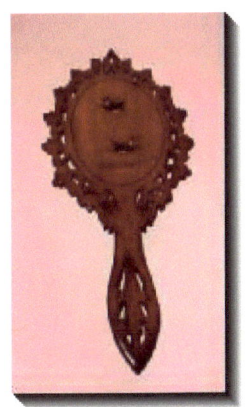
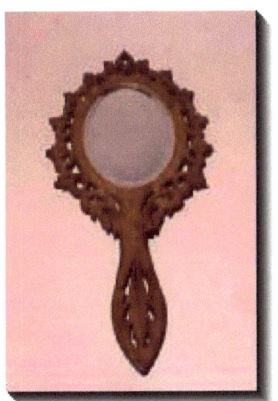
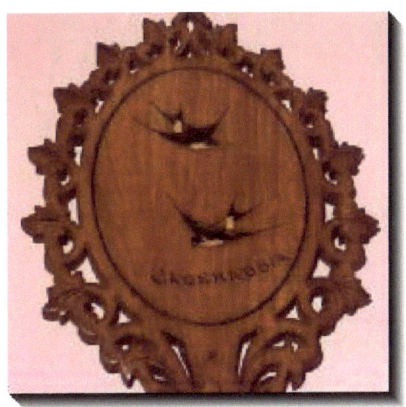
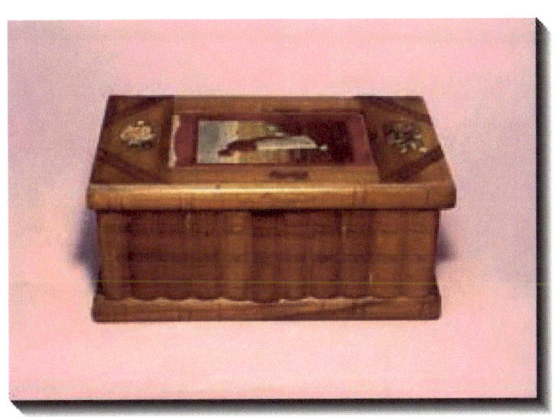

11. Porcelain and Pottery

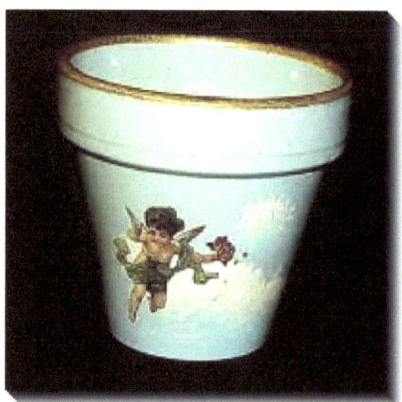

Israeli hand made flower pot, 1940-50, signed "Avoda Ivrit" (Hebrew work/made).

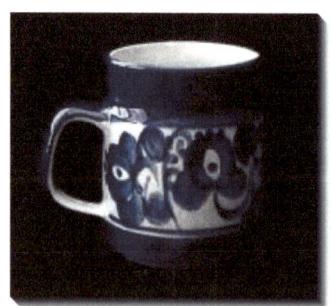

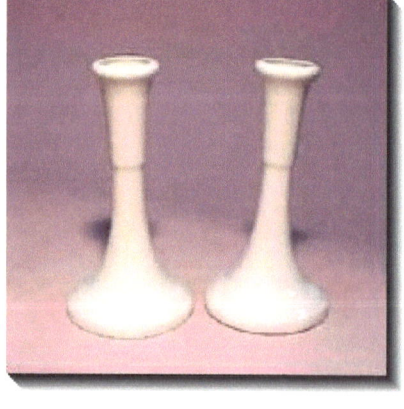

Made by Lapid, Israel 1950/60

Israeli hand made serving plate ceramics, made by "Hutsot Hayotzer"

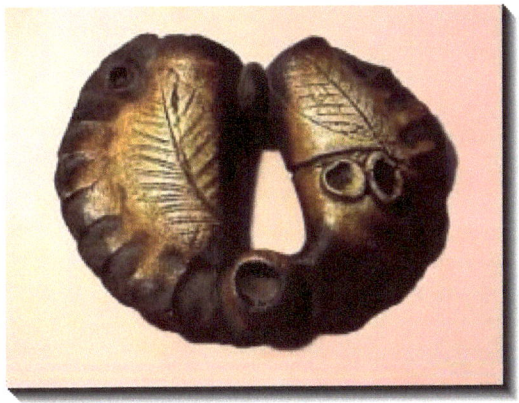

Hand made pottery, shape of ancient water jug, 1950s by "Hai-Israel"

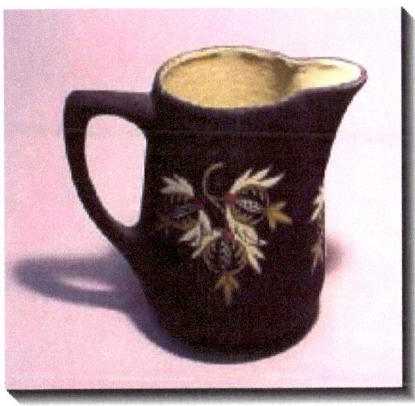

Israeli pottery, hand made pitcher, made in 1950s

A pair of antique Austrian vases, circa 1890.

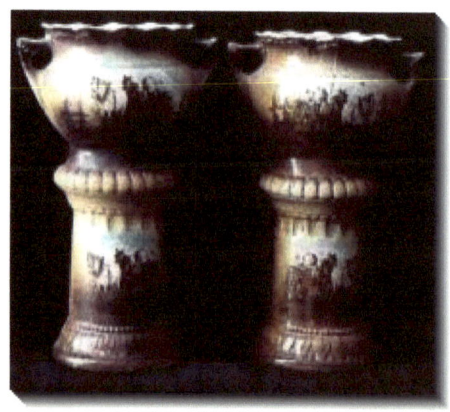

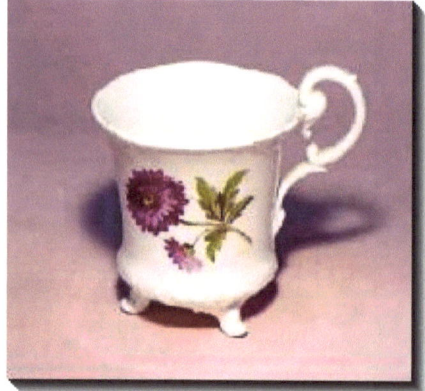

Meissen, Germany, early 20C.

A Japanese huge Imari porcelain plate, gorgeous hand painting.

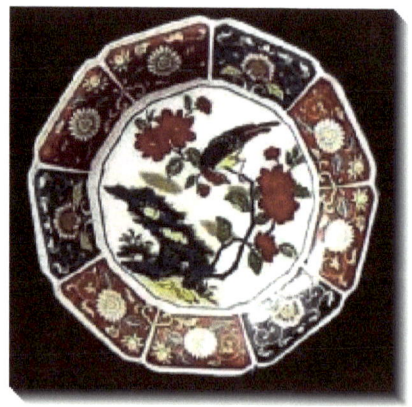

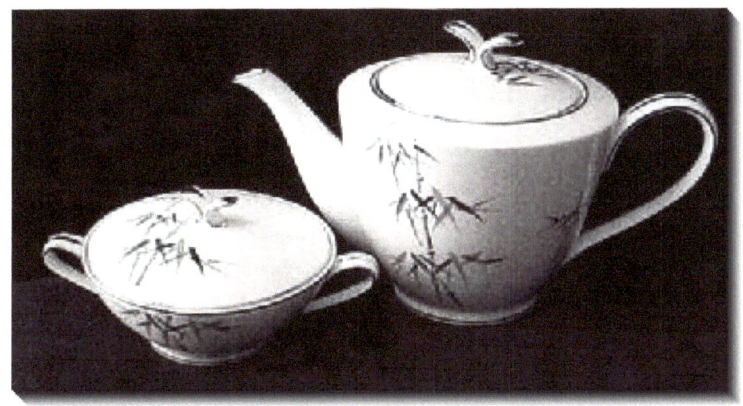

Noritake, tea pot and sugar bowl, pattern Bamboo # 2133.

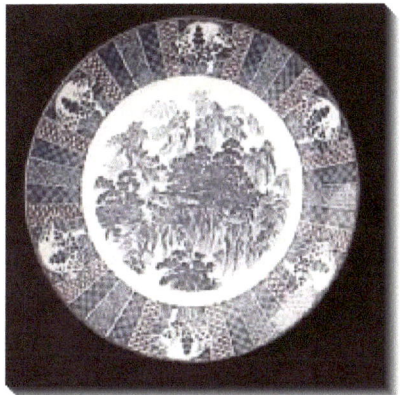

Japanese hand painted plate.

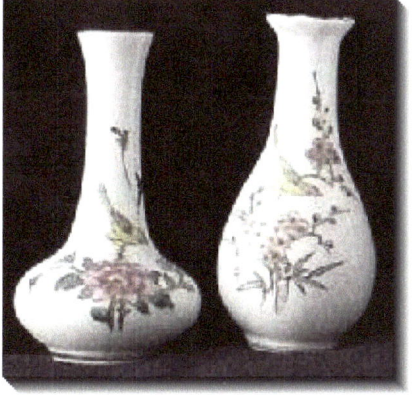

A Pair of Chinese hand painted vases.

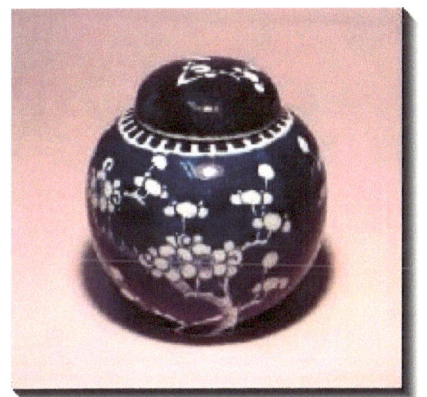

19C Chinese ginger jar decorated with prunus and stems. Blue circle kangxi style mark to the base.

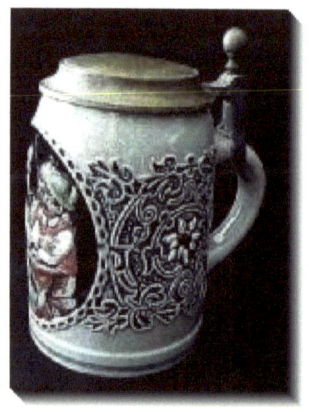 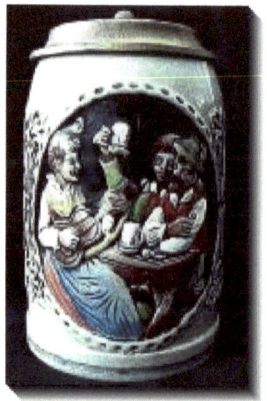

German beer stein, original King, signed and numbered - 403

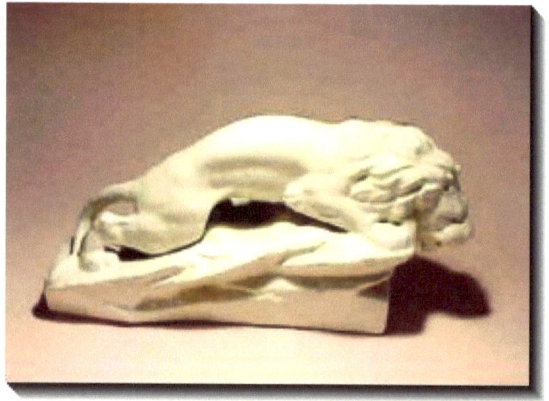

A fine white porcelain large lion, signed RAKO 1933

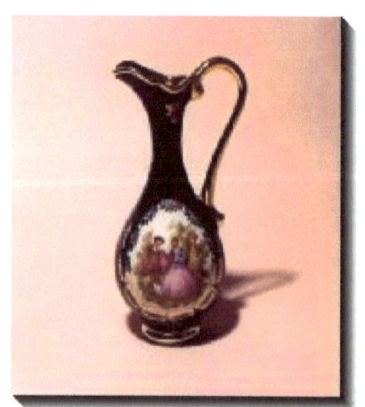

A hand painted porcelain vase, Limoges, France.

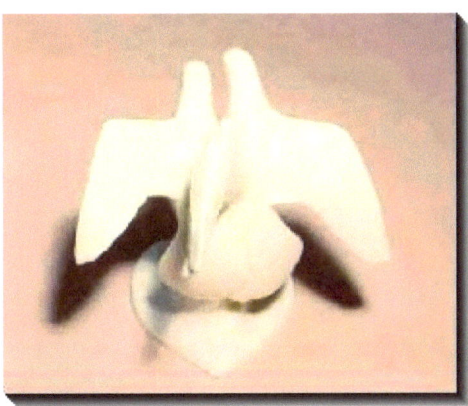

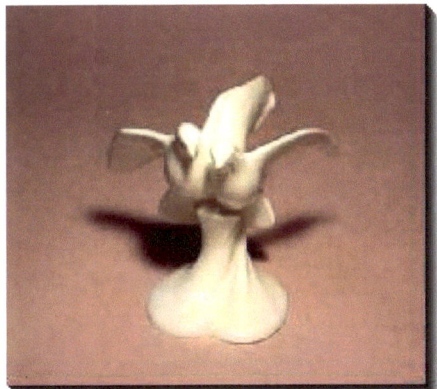

A gorgeous Royal Doulton hand made bone china.

Images of Nature, HN 3550, Modeled and signed by Adrian Hughes 1993-First year of issue.

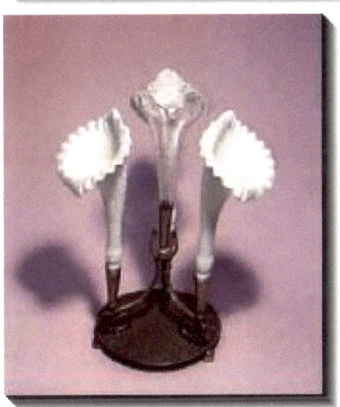

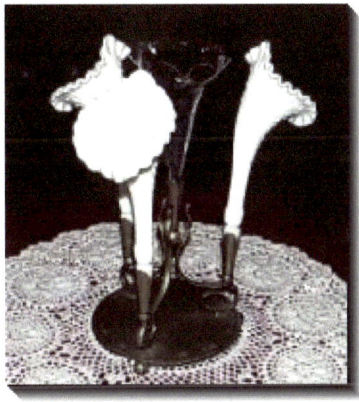

A gorgeous combination of an epergne set made from an English Victorian silver plated base, three original American Fenton white hobnails horns and a 19C Italian gorgeous epergne crystal horn.

Another unusual and rare combination made by the author is the following epergne style item.

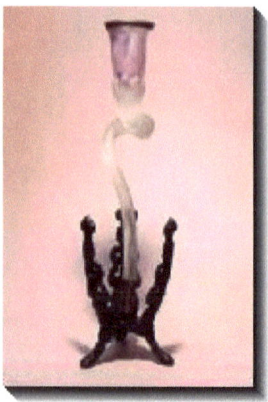

The glass part was found in France, a gorgeous 19th Century made piece, and the heavy metal base was found in England.

12. Islamic and Persian Antiques

Some of the items displayed here were purchased during my trips to the Middle-East, including hunting for antiques at Bazaars in Tehran in the late 1970s.

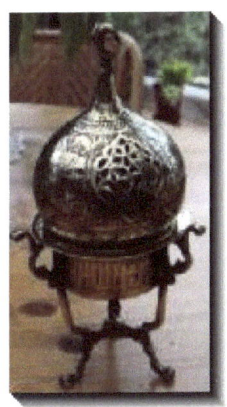
19C Mamluk style Islamic brass incense burner censer.

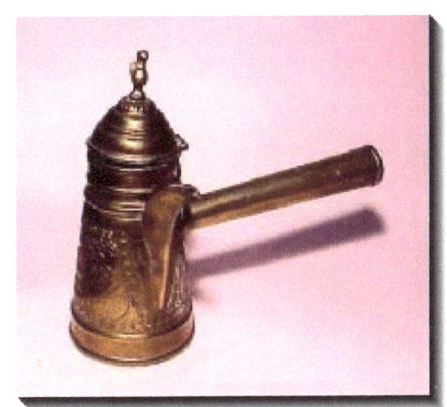
Handcrafted Coffee-Pot by Iskandar Matar from Nazareth.

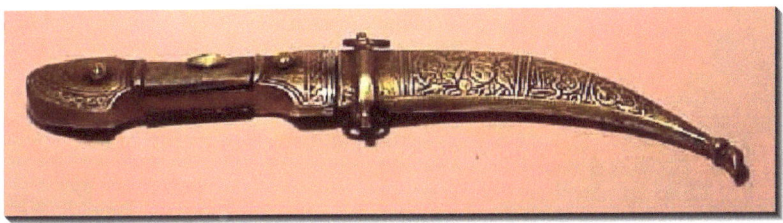
A brass Islamic dagger made in Syria.

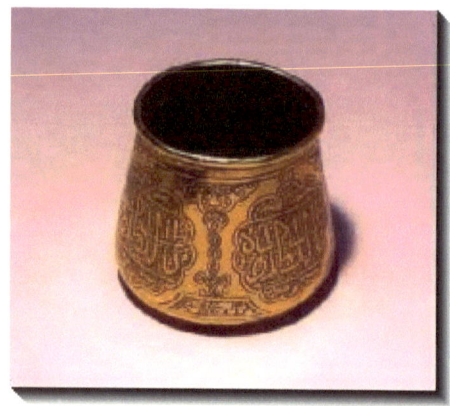

A rare 19C Islamic bowl with beautiful engravings.

A high quality silver inlaid brass Islamic antique bowl.

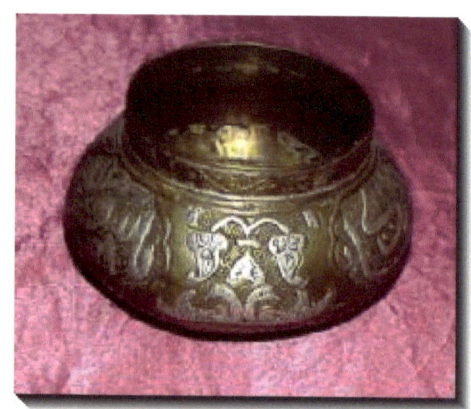

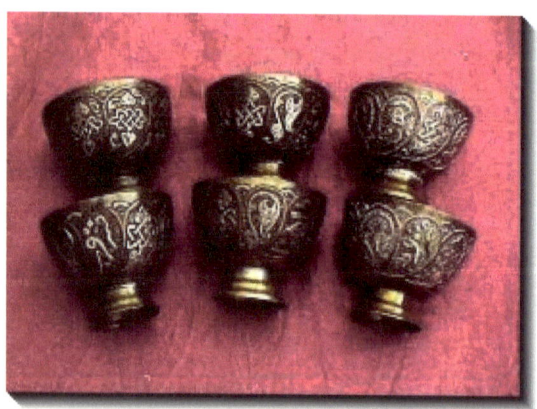

A rare set of six Islamic cups with inlaid silver over brass.

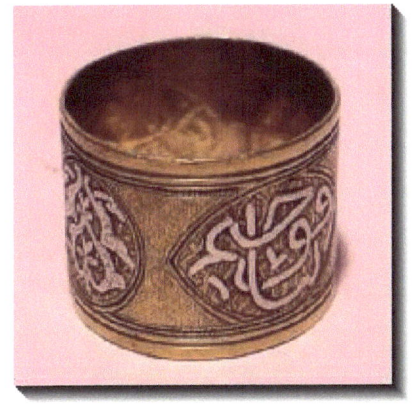

Silver inlaid over brass Islamic napkin holder.

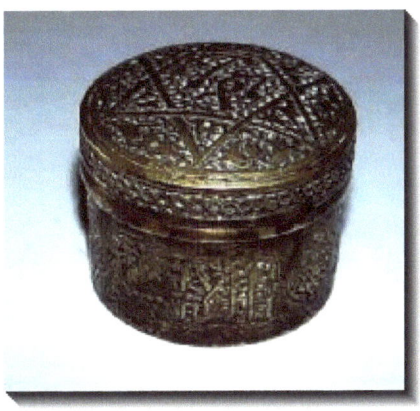

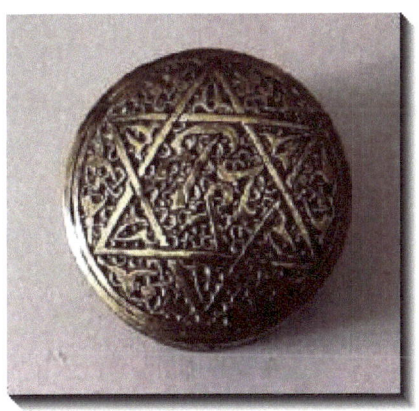

A unique and rare Middle-Eastern 19C brass snuff box with nice engravings.

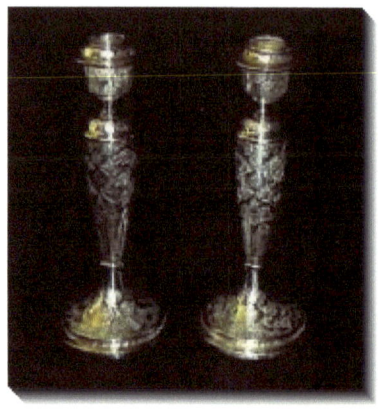 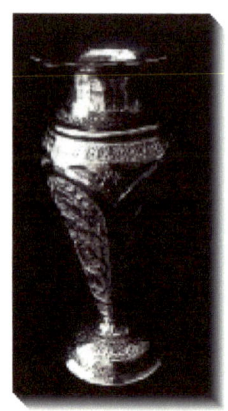

A rare 19C Persian silver candlesticks   A Persian antique vase, 1890

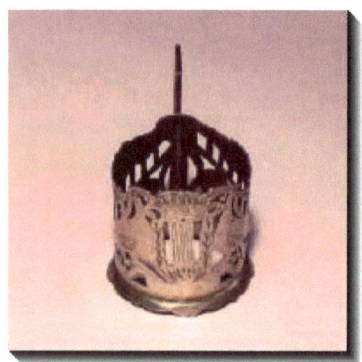 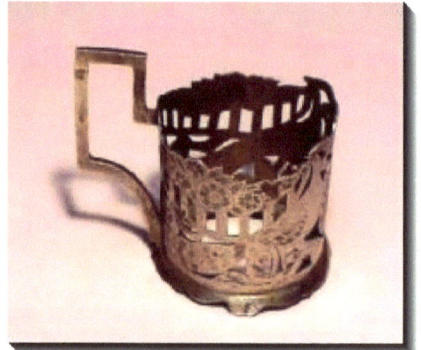

A rare pair of silver (84) 19C Persian cup glass holder.

A gorgeous and rare hand made Persian 19C silver plate.

Maker: Zion Elias, a typical work of art by Jewish silversmith from the 19C.

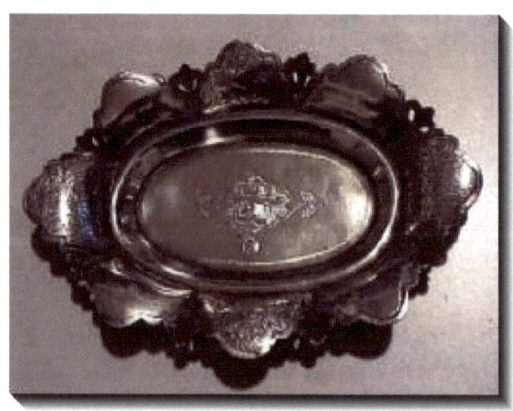

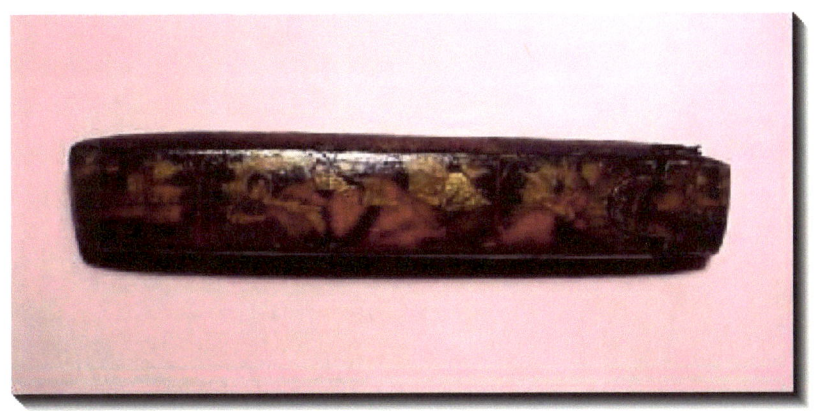

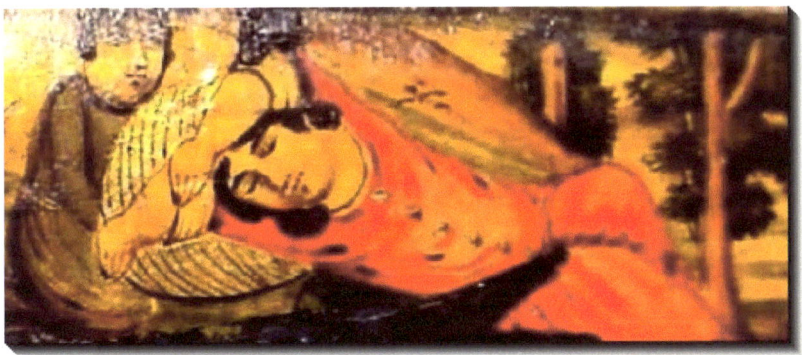

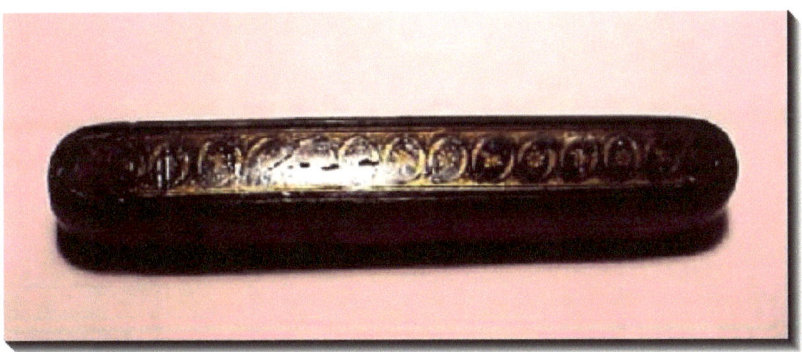

A gorgeous unique and authentic antique Persian paper/papier mâché, Hand painted lacquered pen box - Qalamdan, made about early 1800.

13. Desktop Collectables

Here we present items used on office and home desks such as: inkwells, letter openers, pens and pencils and other desktop related collectables.

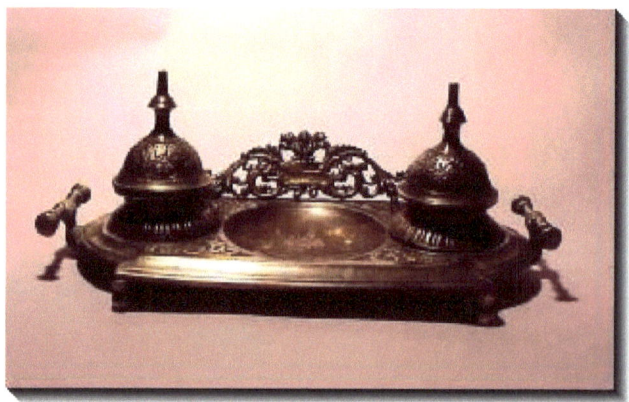

A 19C gorgeous bronze double inkwell.

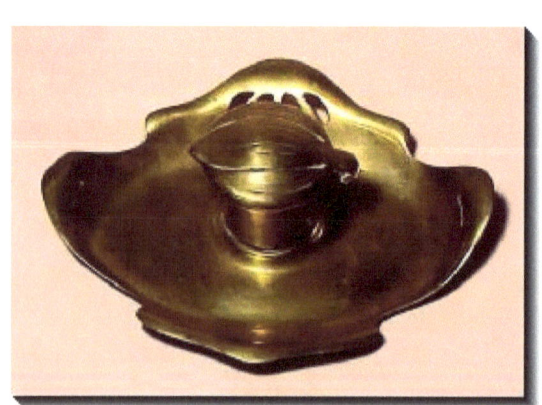

A German Art Nouveau brass inkwell.

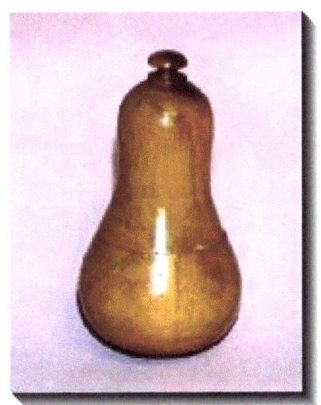

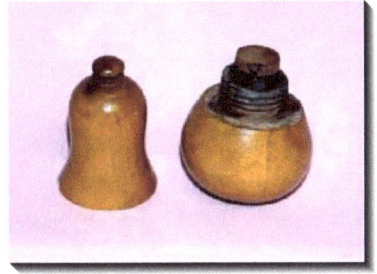

A rare antique olive wood inkwell in the form of a pear, with a blue glass insert, Palestine era.

A hand carved 19C inkwell.

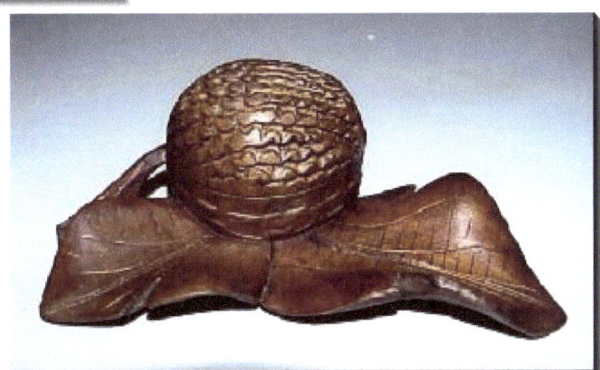

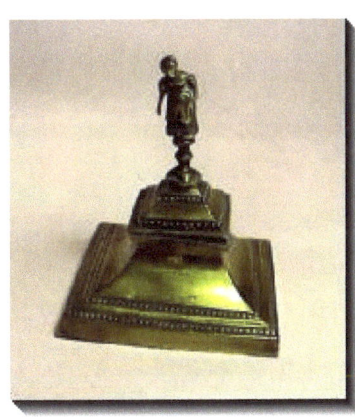

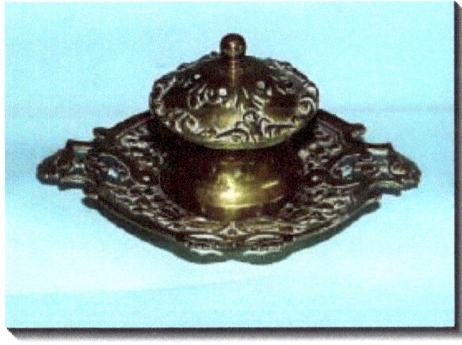

Bronze Victorian English inkwells.

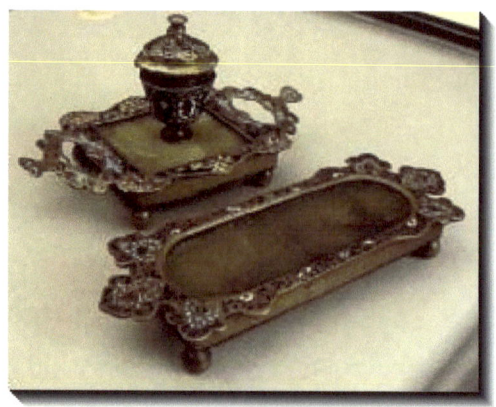

A rare 19C French bronze Champleve inkwell set
Inkwell and tray with onyx/marble base with inlaid enamel.

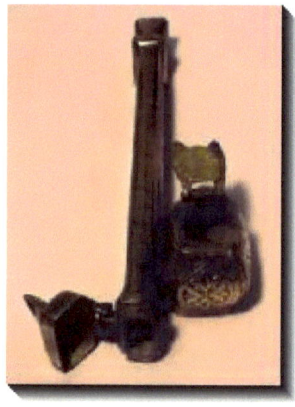

An antique travel brass inkwell, late 19C-early 20C, Middle-Eastern.
This is a scribe's or calligrapher's pen and inkwell case, made of brass, with a compartment to hold quills and ink attachments.

Note: Qalandans have been used in the Middle-East since the 15th Century. There are qalandans with engraved quotations from the Koran in silver and gold inlay, but the majority are brass pen/feather holders, with or without attached ink containers. The ink was often in powdered form.

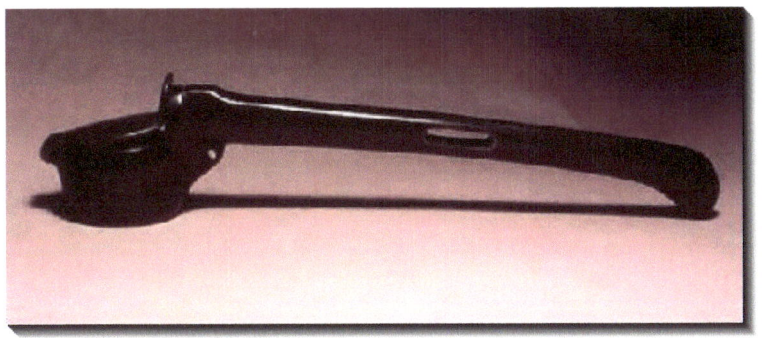

Yatate, Japanese brass inkwell, made about 1880 (Meiji), rare size.

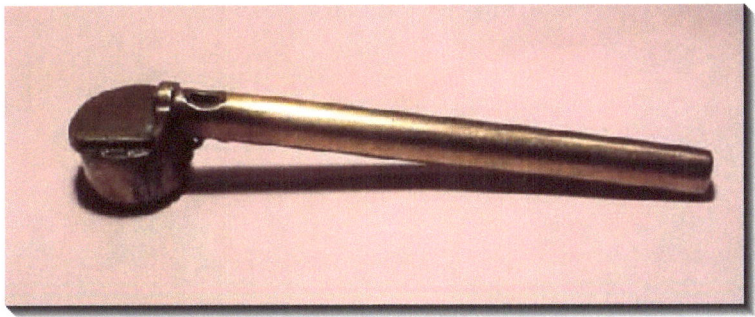

Yatate, Japanese brass inkwell, made before 1920.

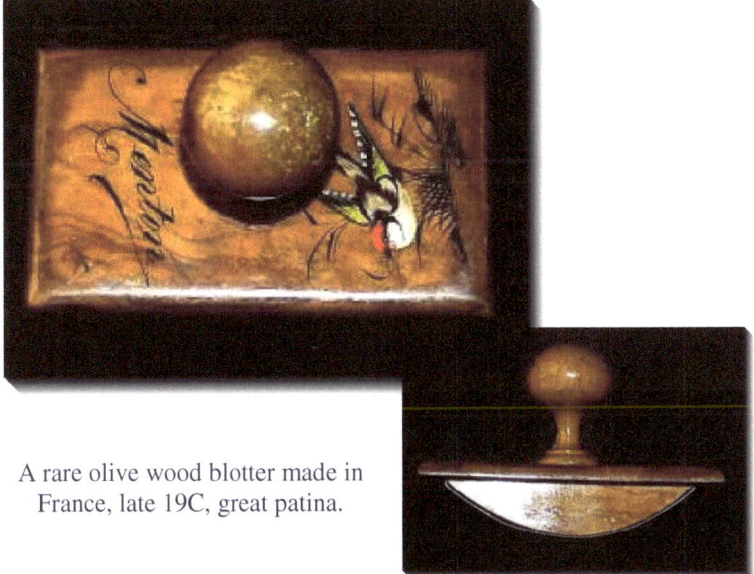

A rare olive wood blotter made in France, late 19C, great patina.

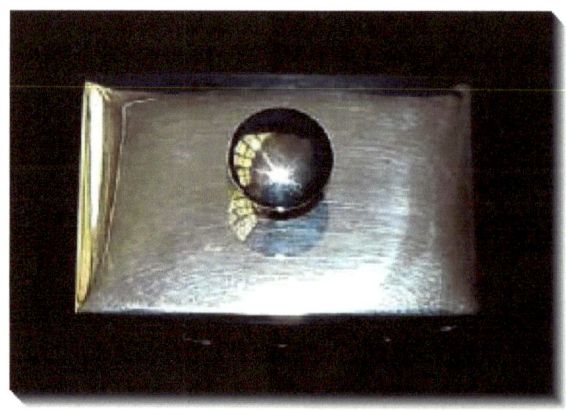

A sterling silver English blotter.

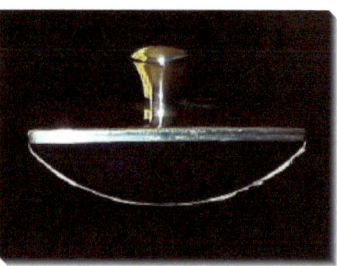

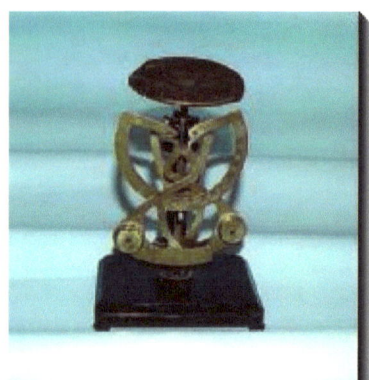

A German letter scale by
Columbus Bilateral.
Patented 1904-6

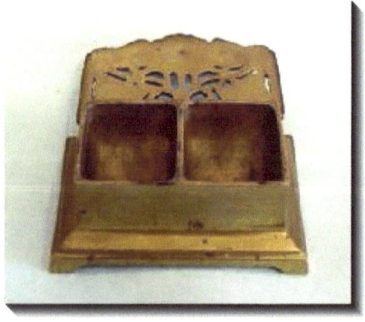

A Victorian brass stamp holder.

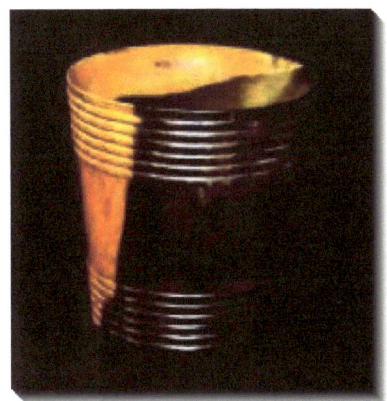 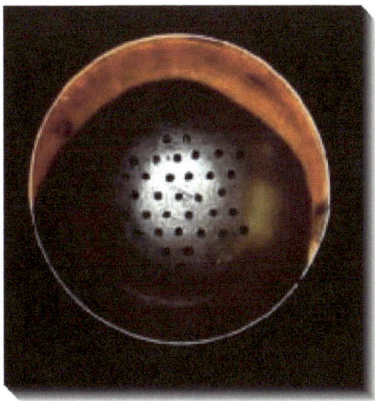

A beautiful and extremely rare 19C ink sander, made of Lignum Vitae.
The holes form a Star of David.

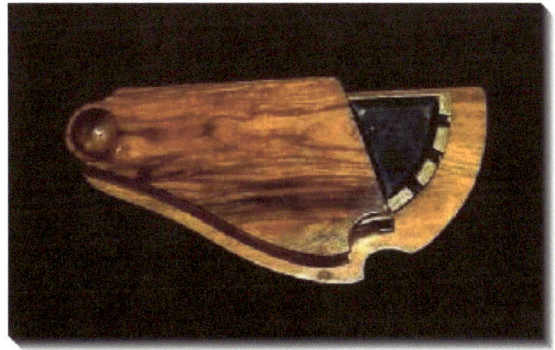

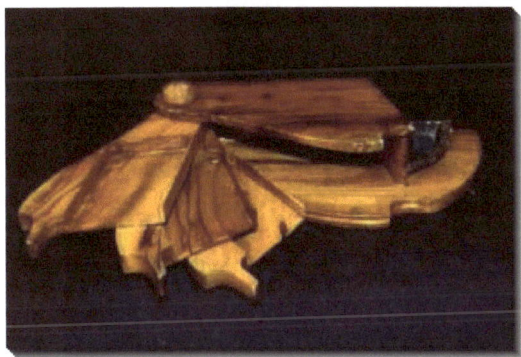

An olive wood desktop in shape of harp, Israel 1950s.

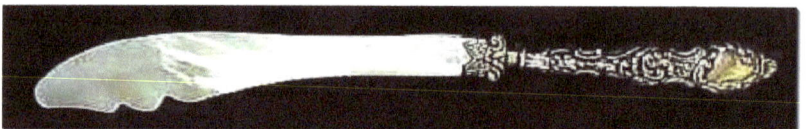

A gorgeous sterling silver and mother of pearl Art Nouveau letter opener.

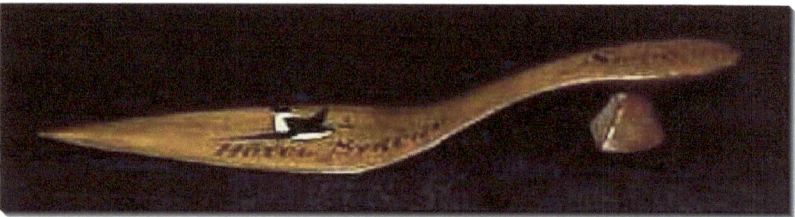

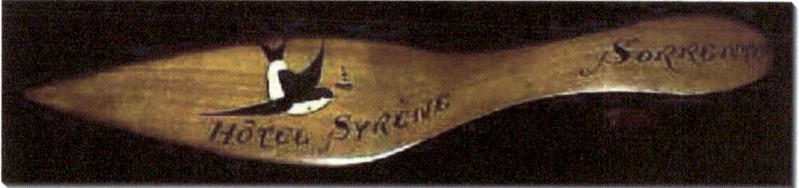

A gorgeous and rare handmade wooden letter opener in the form of lady's shoe.

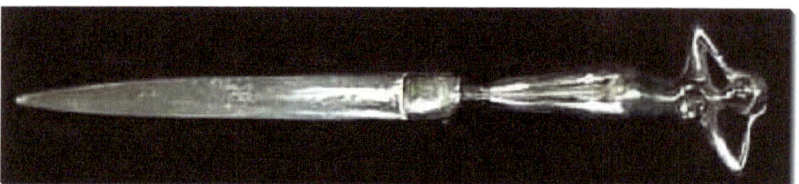

An Art Nouveau silver plated heavy letter opener, early 20C.

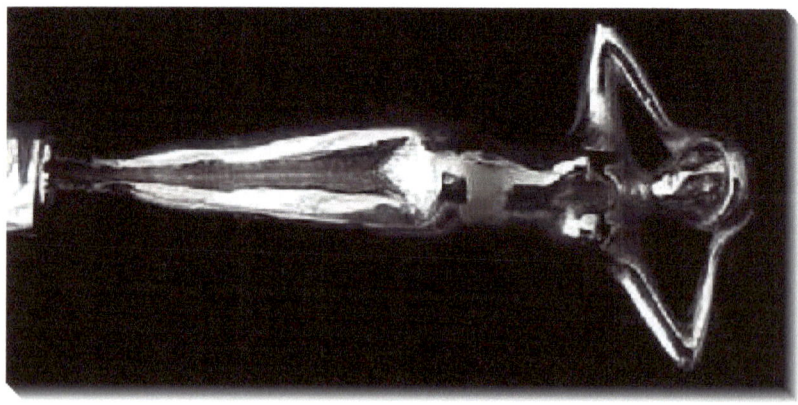

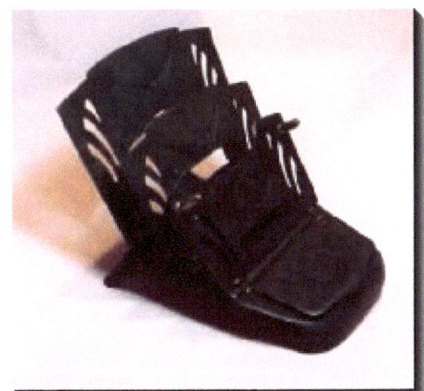
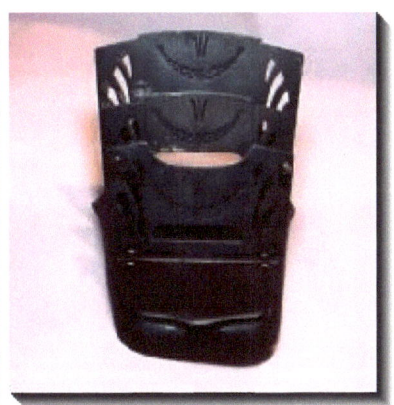
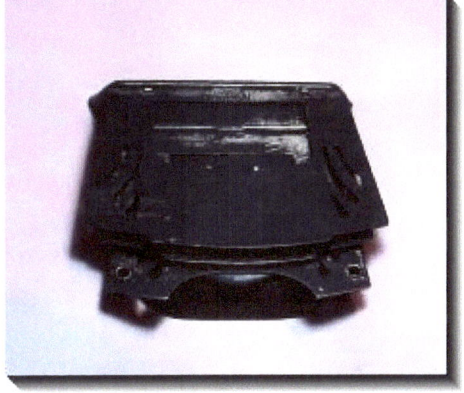

A rare German art nouveau (1904-7) folding letter and stamp stand Marked D.R.G.M. (Deutsches Reich Gebrauch Muster) 237679.

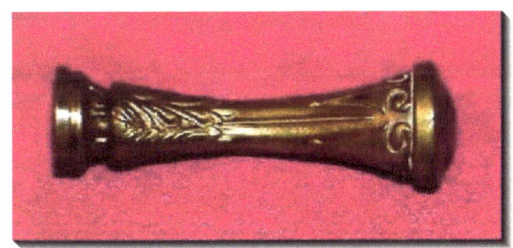

A Victorian brass wax seal with removable brass stamp

A rare Victorian wax seal with removable brass stamp. Handle made of Lignum Vitae.

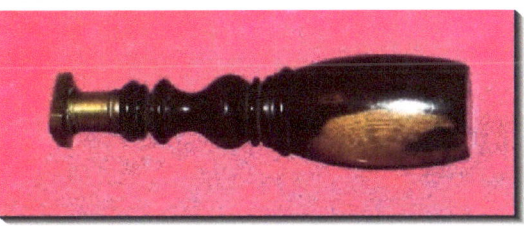

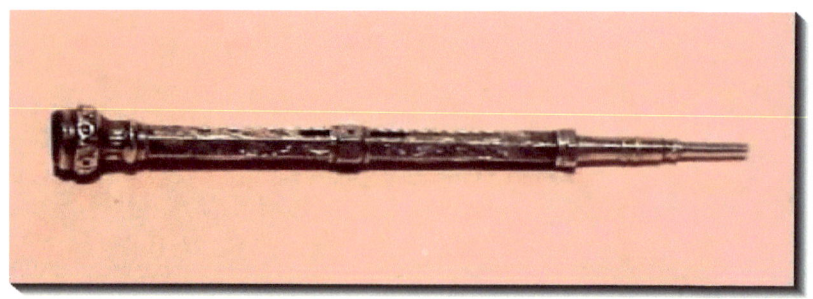

A beautiful sterling silver pencil made in Chester England in 1894

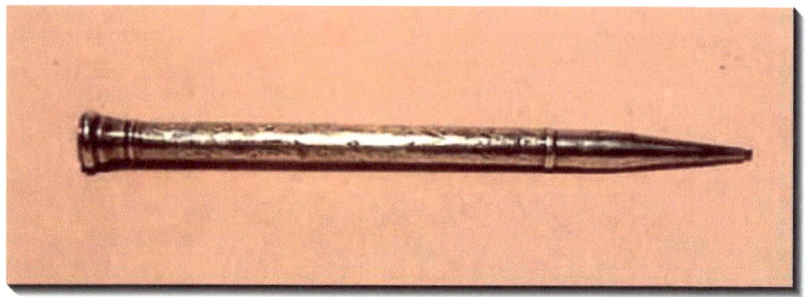

Mordan Everpoint sterling silver pencil, made in England in 1934.

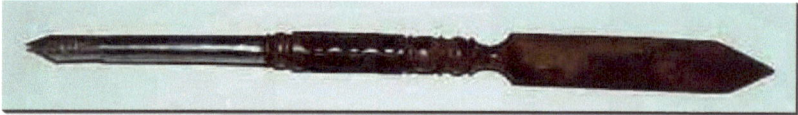

A rare late 19C antique Stanhope dip pen and letter opener, made of olive wood, using photo-micrographic techniques showing views of Jerusalem.

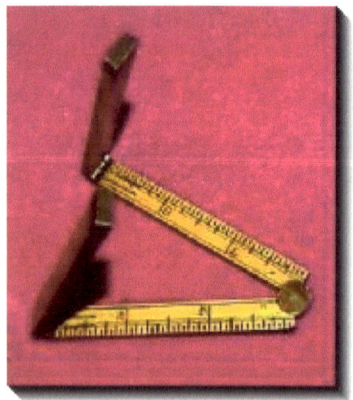

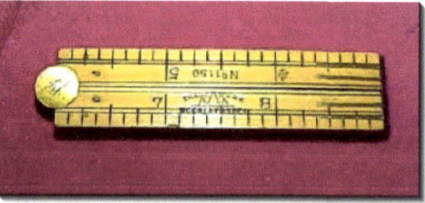

A 12" (1 foot) folding boxwood rule by Hockley Abbey, made in England, #1150

14. Tobacciana and Boxes

In this category, we have, in addition to the classical tobacciana collectables such as pipes and related items, also cigarette and snuff boxes, mainly made of silver and they are highly collectable.

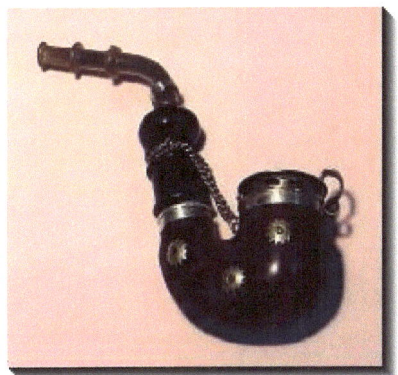
Pipe by Bruyer Garantie

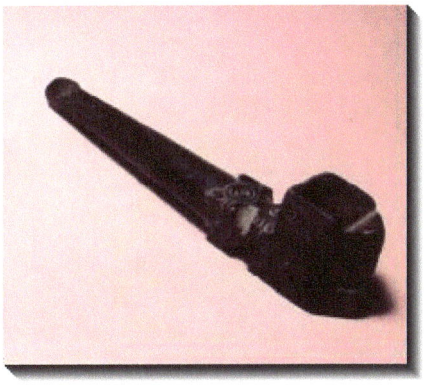
Stone carved 19C pipe/cigarette holder.

A beautifully carved vintage pipe head with inlaid meerschaum.

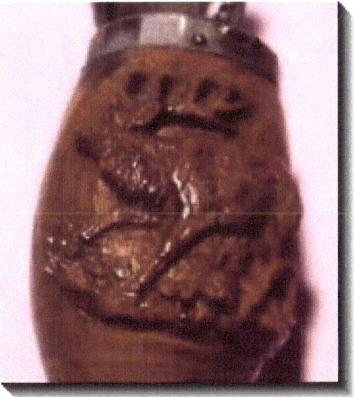

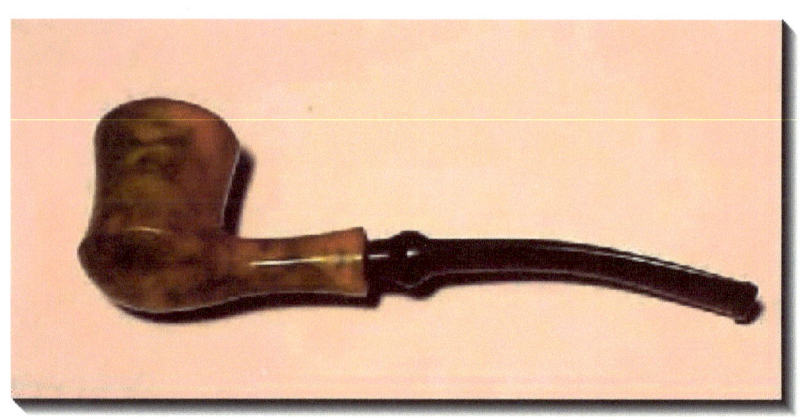

Pipe by Hilson #202 with inlaid meerschaum

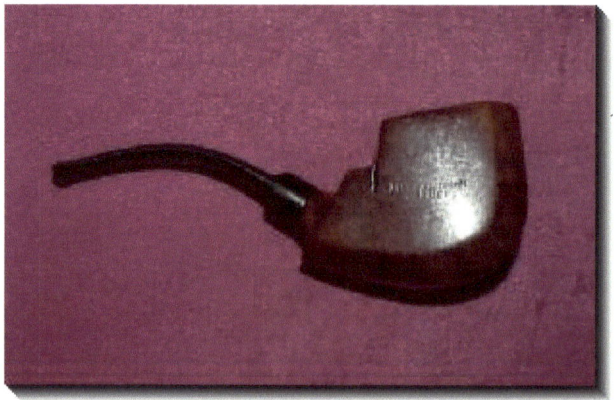

French pipe, Algerian briar

Italian pipe rack for four pipes in a unique Pyramid design.

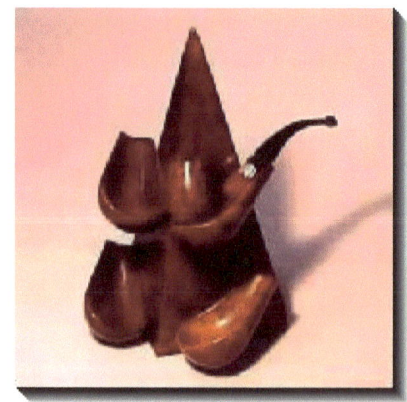

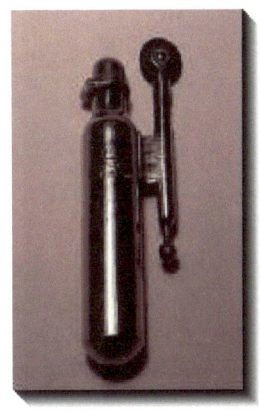
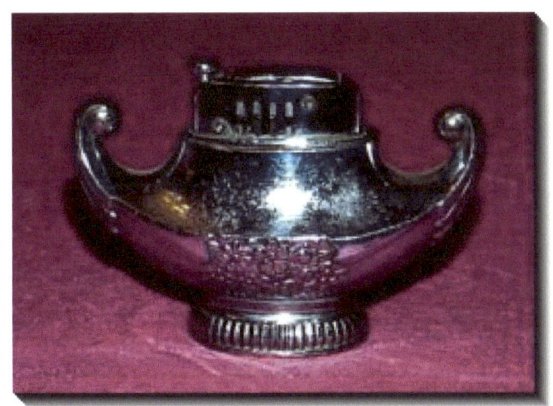

A rare Austrian early 20C petrol lighter.

Aladdin/Genie's lamp style lighter, "Made in Occupied Japan" (1945)

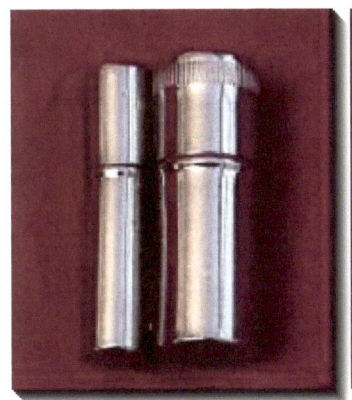
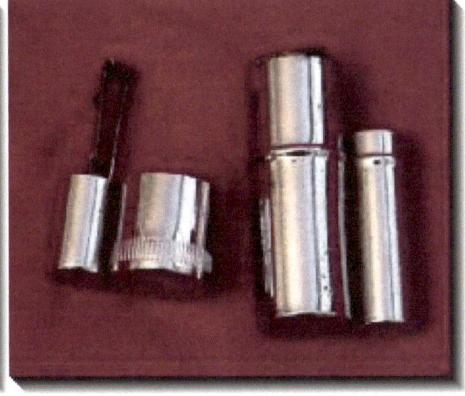

A rare self starting catalytic lighter by New Method Co. Bradford, PA.

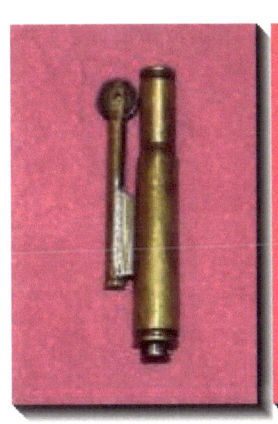
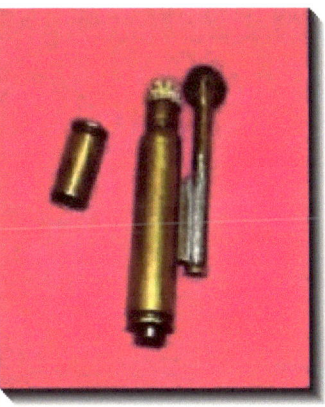

A rare Trench Art lighter, made from bullet, marked: K 30 67

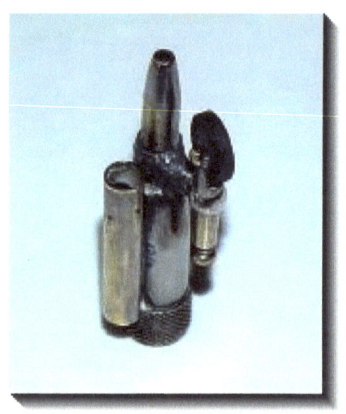 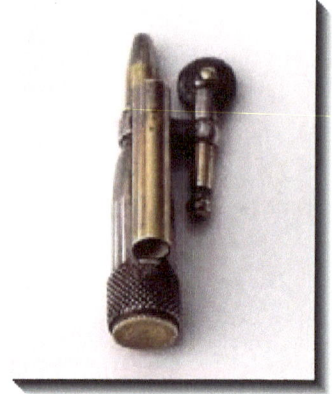

A unique and rare Trench-Art WWI petrol lighter.

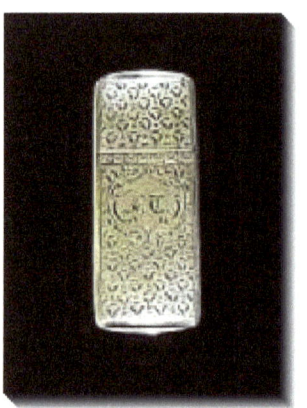 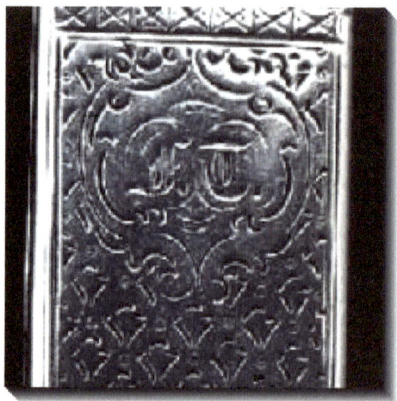

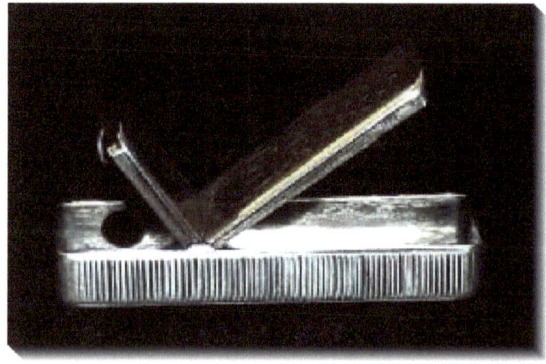

A superb and rare 19C Austro-Hungarian silver (old Vienna mark) Match / Snuff box, made in 1854.

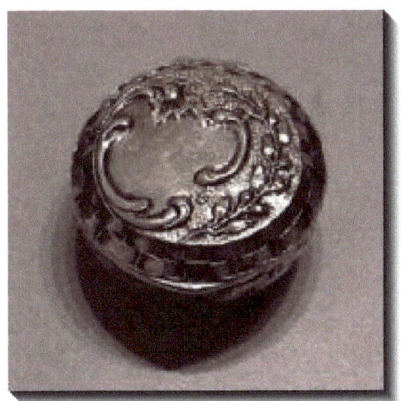

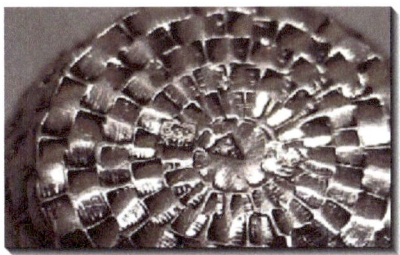

A rare silver (800) snuff-pill box, it has the mark of the Brussels workshop, Wolfers' Frères (triangle with 3 stars) and the German Reich mark (export).

A rare antique snuff box, on the cover "Saint George slaying the dragon" and the text: *Honi soit qui mal y pense* meaning: Shamed be he who thinks evil of it - Edward III, Rex Britania, AD1348.

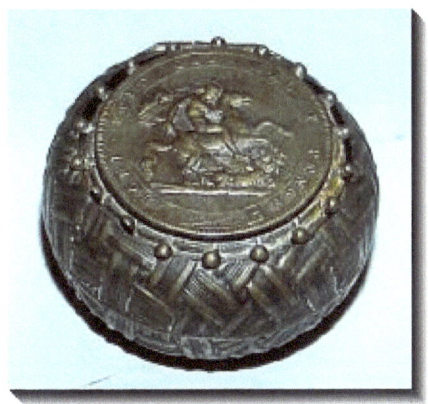

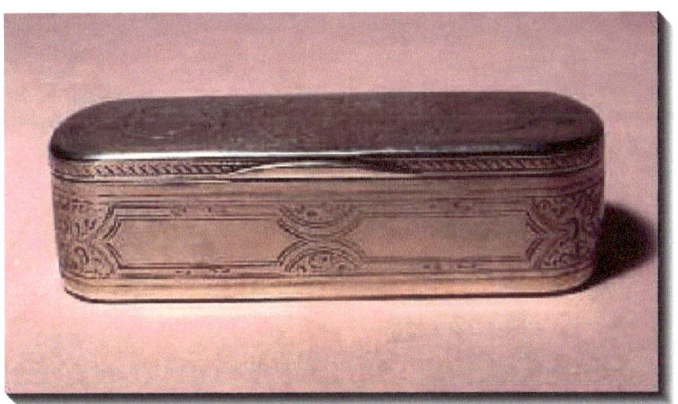

A superb 19C Austro-Hungarian silver (old Vienna mark) Snuff box, made in 1850.

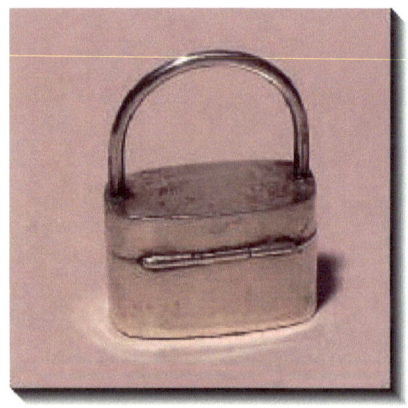
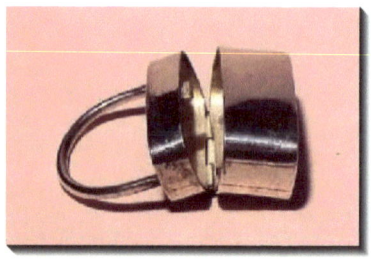

A special sterling silver pill box in shape of a lock, made in Mexico.

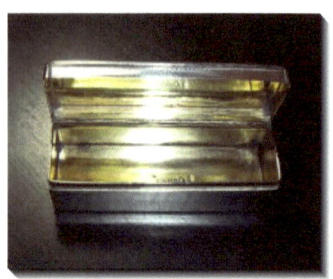
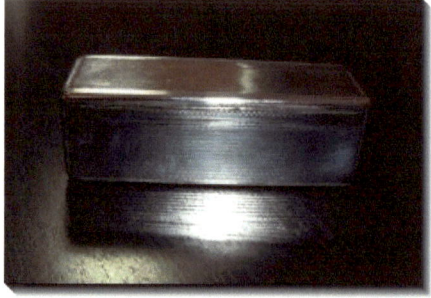

A superb sterling silver snuff box made in 1822 (George IV), London England, maker WE (William Eley).

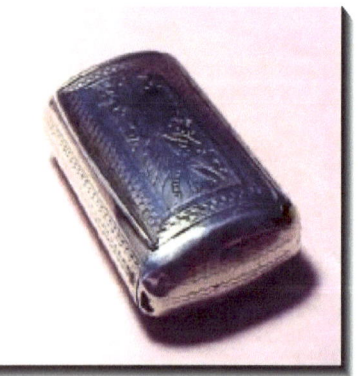
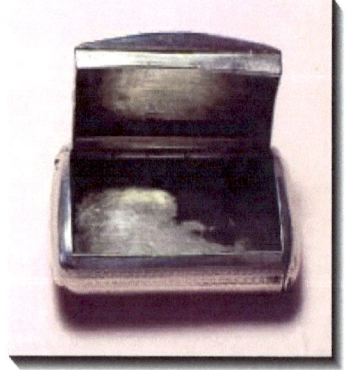

A rare 19C silver snuff box made by the famous French silver maker Lucien Boulard (1866-1910).

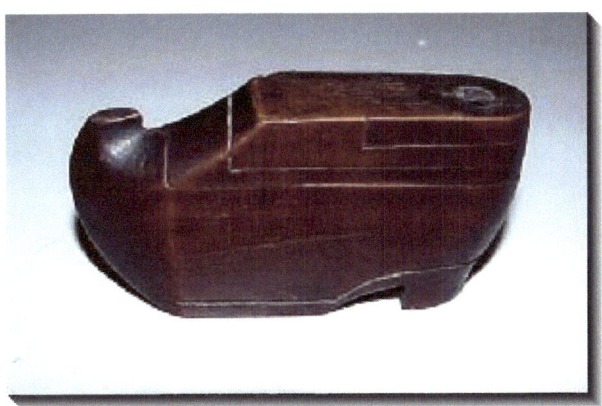

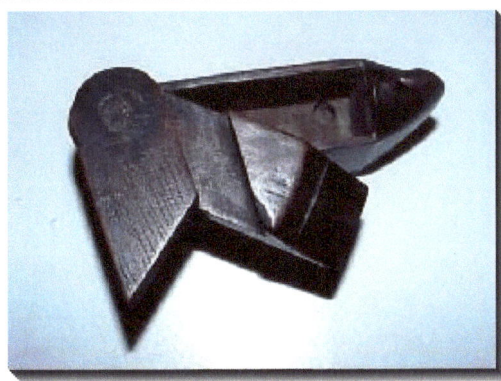

A rare 19C wooden treen shoe-shaped snuff box, England.

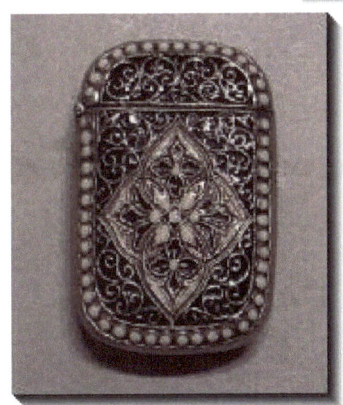

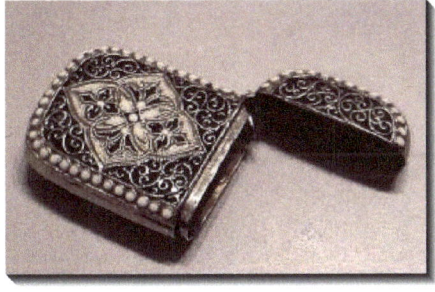

Norwegian Silver and Enamel Vesta Case by David Andersen, Norway 1888 – 1925.

This is a beautiful and rare vesta case by the Norwegian silversmith, David Andersen. The early David Andersen mark of bench tools is on the rim inside the lid.

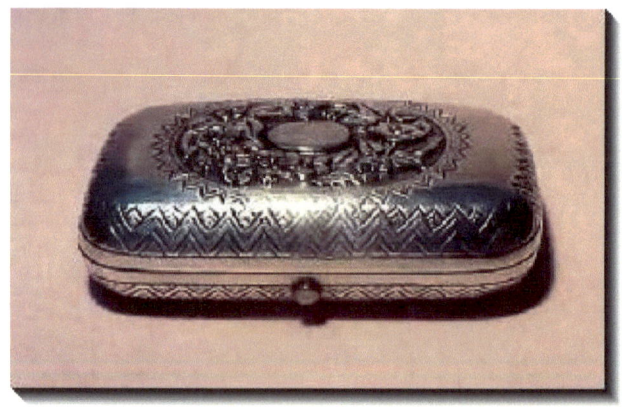

A gorgeous Russian heavy silver (84) snuff/cigarette box made in 1882.

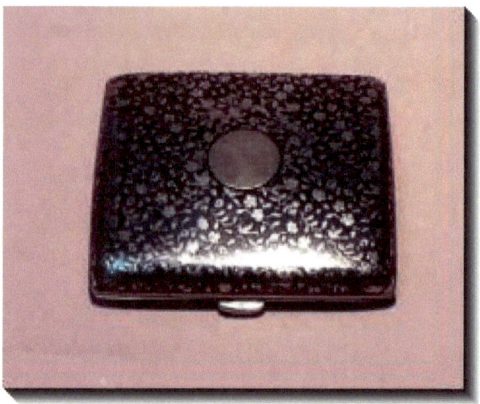

A 19C Hungarian silver (800) and Niello (birds & flowers) cigarette box.

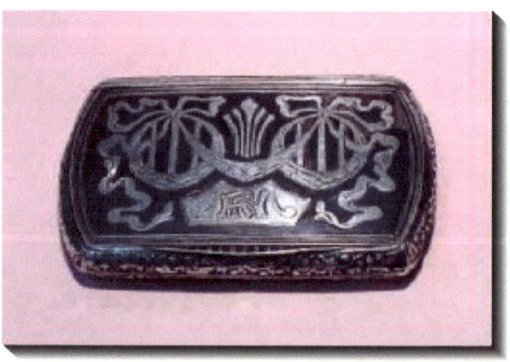

A 19C Hungarian silver (900) and Niello cigarette box, maker F.B.

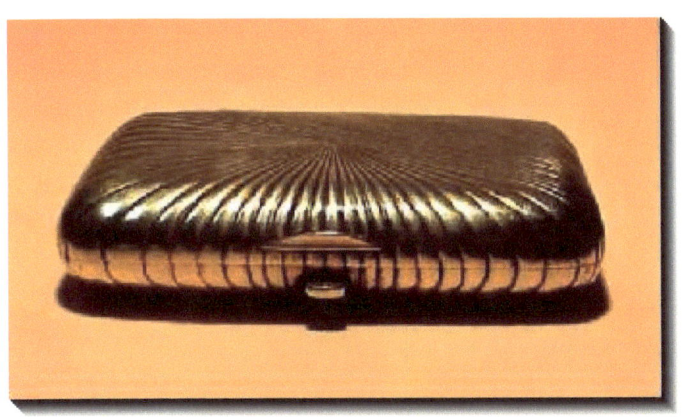

A rare 19C Imperial Russian silver (84) cigarette box.

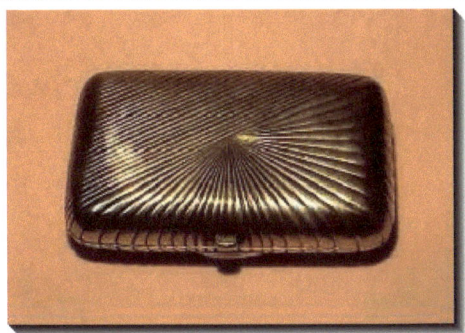

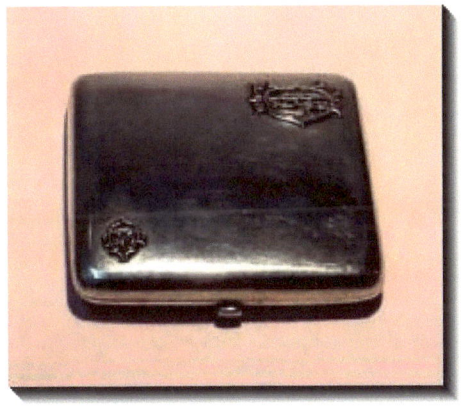
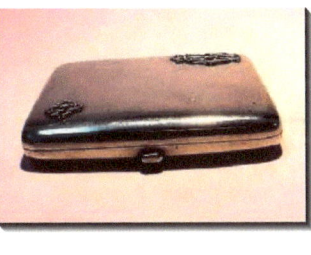

A 19C Imperial Russian heavy silver (84) cigarette box.

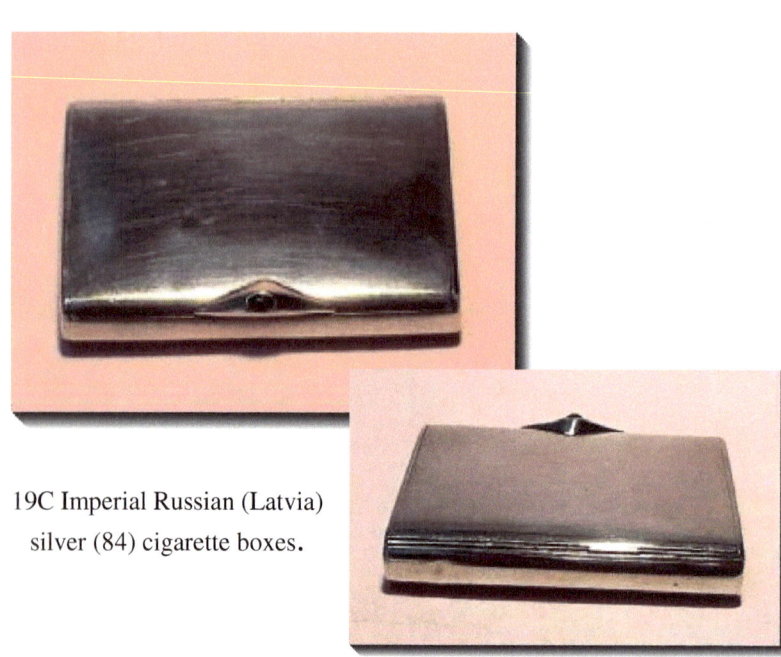

19C Imperial Russian (Latvia) silver (84) cigarette boxes.

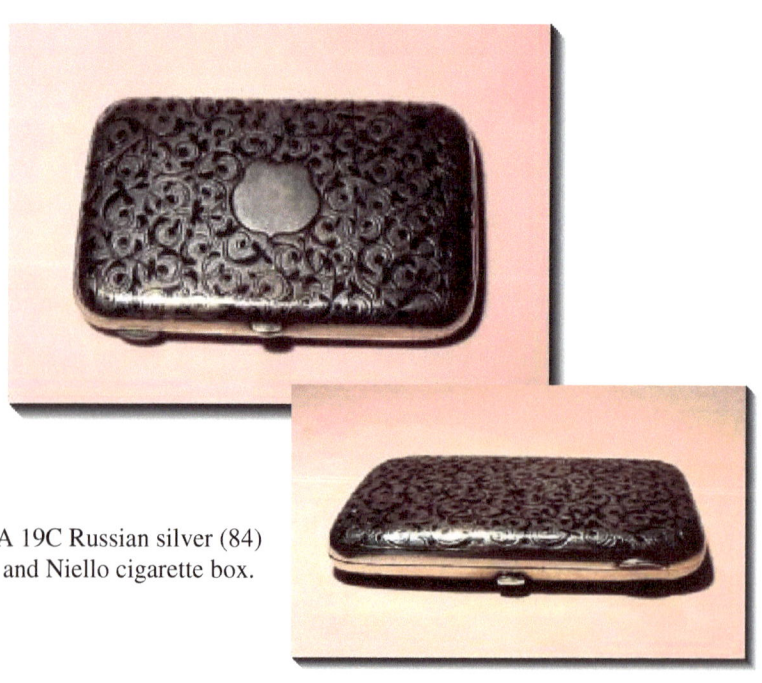

A 19C Russian silver (84) and Niello cigarette box.

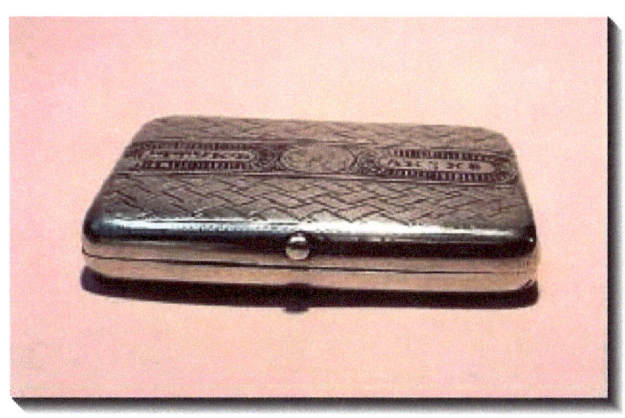

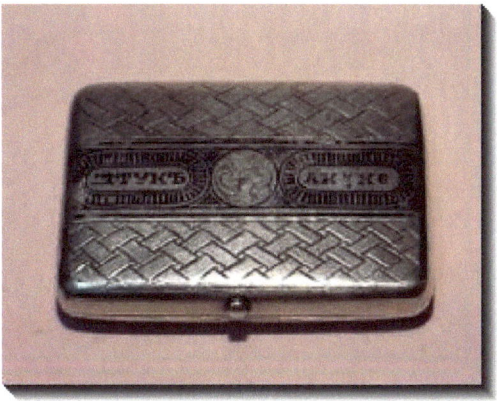

This unique box is imperial Russian silver (84) and Niello cigarette case, made in Moscow in 1895.

Assayed by Oleks Lev Fedorovich 1890-1896 (Post.-Loseva, #2121, 2122), Made by Pokrovskij Tixonov 1868-1897 (Post.-Loseva #2745).

15. Coins and Medals

General coins and medals mainly from Israel are presented here. A few Roman and Hasmonean era coins are also included.

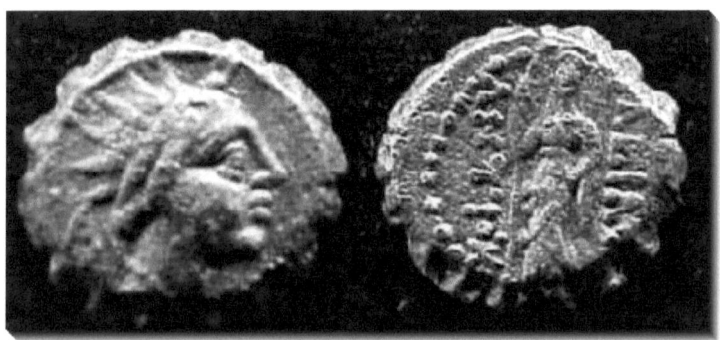

Antiochus (IV or V) Seleucid King of Syria, 138-129 BCE., The obverse is the king radiate, the reverse is probably Zeus.

These coins are genuine ancient Roman bronze coins from about 230 BCE and up to the 4th Century CE. They were discovered and auctioned in Israel.

Roman ancient coins were hand made by inserting a metal blank between two dies and striking with a hammer, most of them are not perfectly round.

The terms BCE = Before Common Era and CE=Common Era are used instead of BC=Before Christ and AD= *Anno Domini* in Latin or *The Year of the Lord* in English.

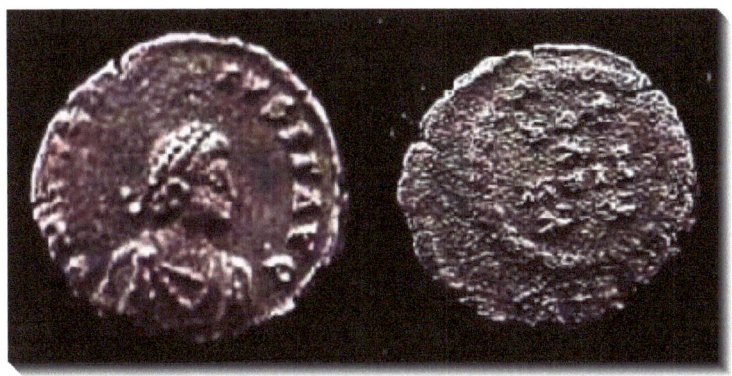

A rare Gratian coin. (Gratian was Roman Emperor from 375 to 383).

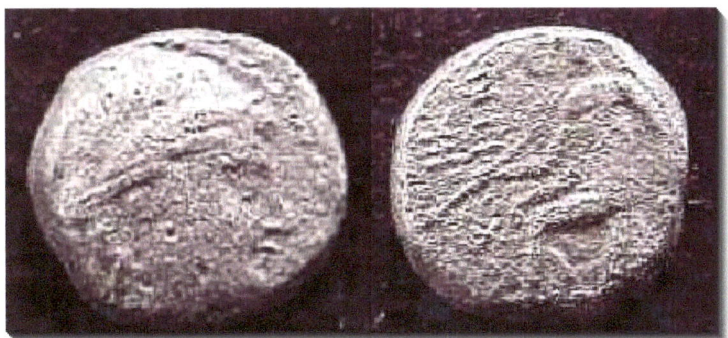

Seleucid Kingdom, Antiochus III, the Great, 223-187 BCE., Sear 6946, Obv: diademed head of Apollo or king; Rev: ΒΑΣΙΛΕΩΣ (off flan left) ΑΝΤΙΟΧΟΥ, in field to left monogram, seated on an omphalos, (religious stone artifact) resting on bow, looking down an arrow.

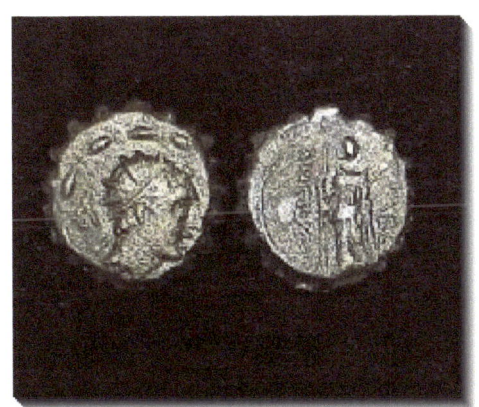

Antiochus IV Seleucid King of Syria, 138-129 BCE.

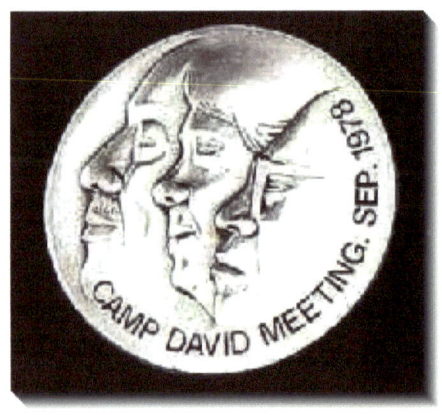
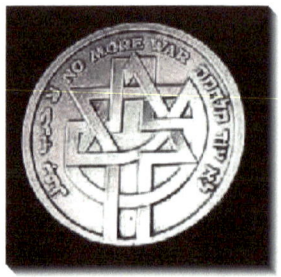

Silver medal, Camp David meeting, 17 September 1978, Issued by the government of Israel, no. 2089.

Bronze medal, 'Bar-Mitzvah' Issued by the State of Israel.

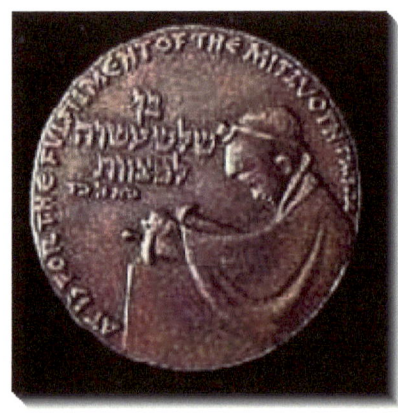

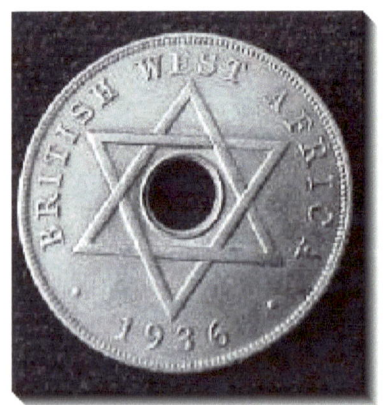

British West Africa, 1936, King Edward VIII, One Penny.

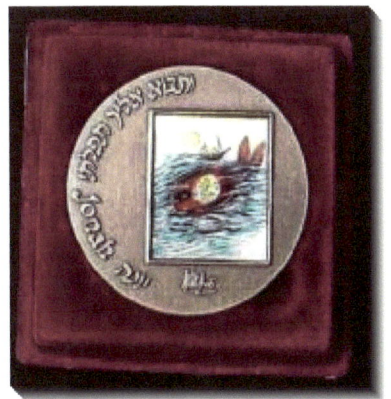

A unique bronze medal, with a picture (enamel) by the famous artist Reuven Rubin with his signature on both sides.

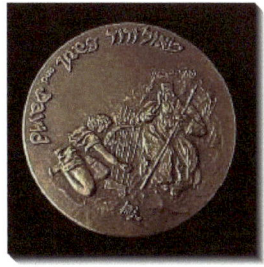

The picture shows Jonah inside the wale. Side-1 - 'Vatavo Elecha Tefilati'='My Prayers will come to you' -Jonah, Side-2 - Saul and David. On rim: Bronze, State of Israel, number 0422.

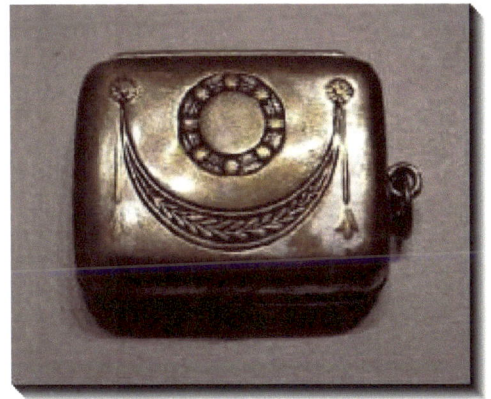

A bronze medal, issued by the State of Israel. Prime Minister Yitzhak Rabin.1922-1995.

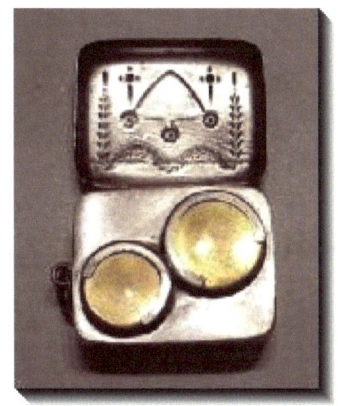

A rare Art Nouveau silver plated coin box.

16. Jewellery and Watches

Diverse, simple, and low cost vintage jewellery items such as: bracelets, brooches, pins, compacts, earrings, necklaces, pendants, rings are presented in the *Antiques Online Catalogue*. In addition, certain watches and antique chains are also included in this category. Here I show just a sample from that collection.

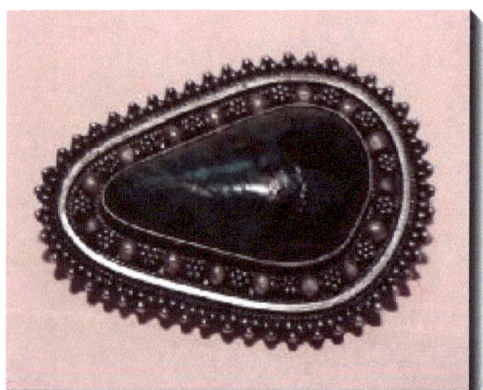

A unique sterling silver brooch and pendant, made in Israel during the 1950s by Bezalel.

A gorgeous and rare sterling silver brooch made in Jerusalem during the 1950s by Hans Teppich.

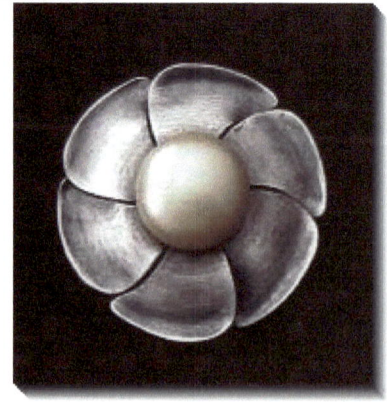

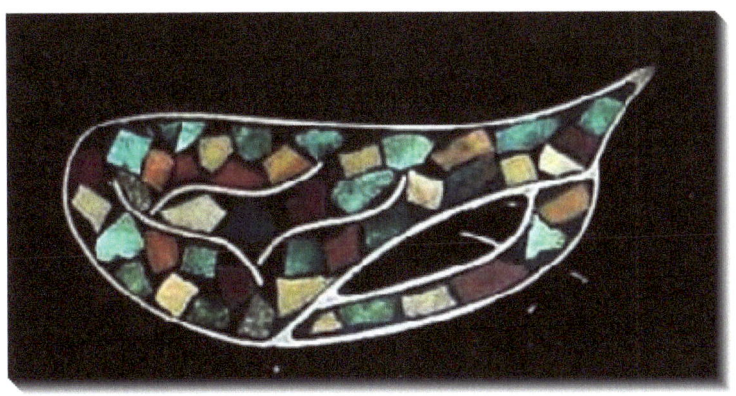

A gorgeous sterling silver brooch and pendant with inlaid color stones, Made in Israel during the 1950s by Bezalel.

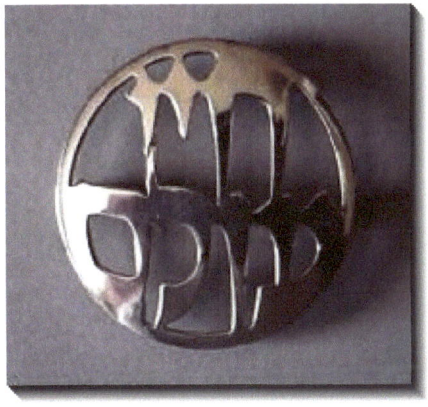

A gorgeous jewellery item, sterling silver pin/brooch, signed by Wolpert. In Hebrew: "Chayey Olam" - "Eternal Life".

Ludwig Yehuda Wolpert was a sculptor and a painter. He was born in Germany. In 1938 he emigrated to Israel. At Bezalel Jerusalem, he was the head of the metal department. He designed and made religious articles. In 1977 he exhibited at the Jewish Museum, New York - "Fifty Years of Jewish Art".

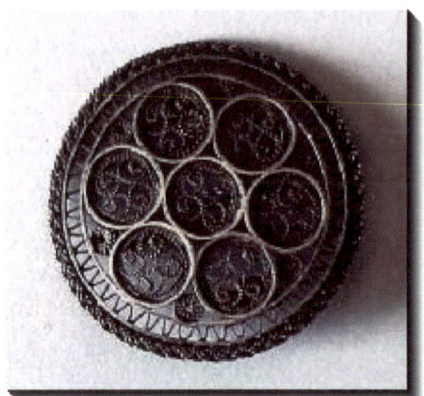 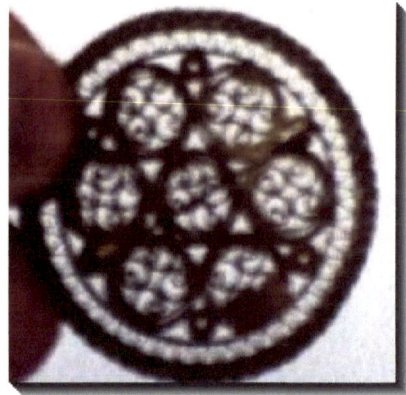

A very rare filigree sterling silver brooch made in Palestine, signed. When viewed from back it 'generates' a "Star of David" as seen.

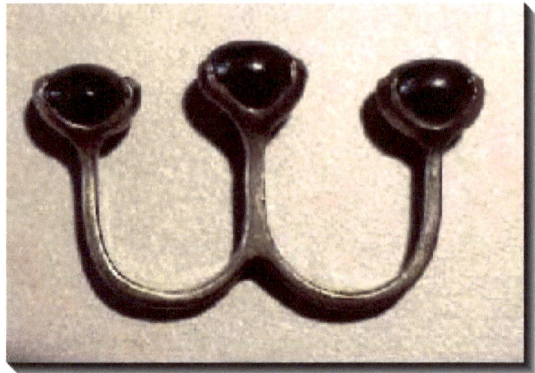

A unique modern double finger sterling silver ring. Made by Yuval from Jerusalem.

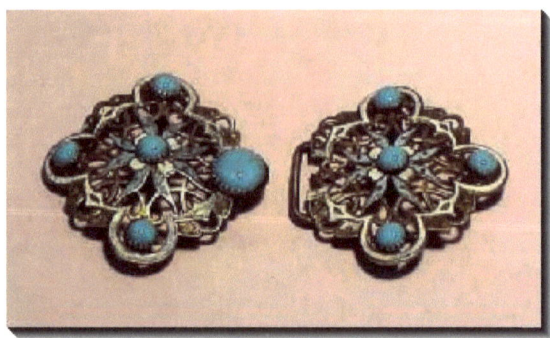

A rare antique Victorian belt buckle set, turquoise stones with enamel.

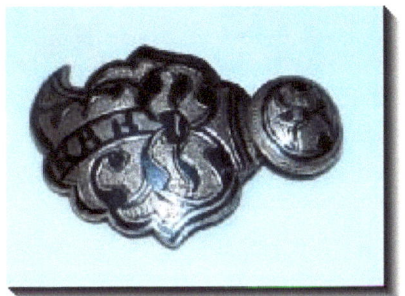

A 19C Russian Caucasus Cossack belt part, made of silver 84 and niello.

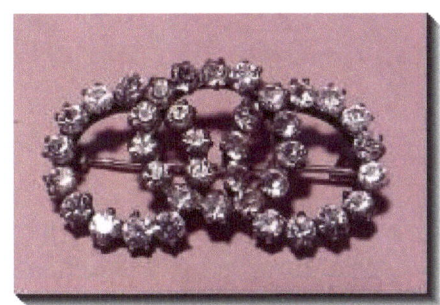

A Russian silver brooch with inlaid Rhine stones.

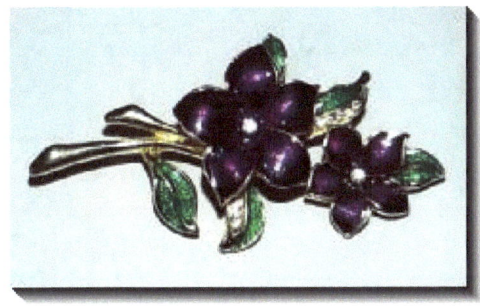

A gorgeous brooch 24K gilded, with inlaid color enamel and Rhine stones.

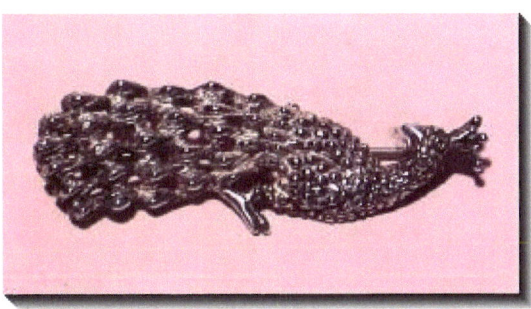

A gorgeous peacock brooch made of sterling silver.

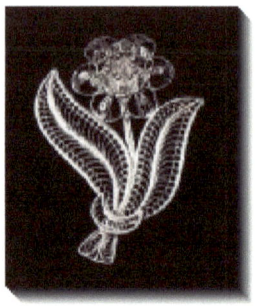
A silver filigree brooch.

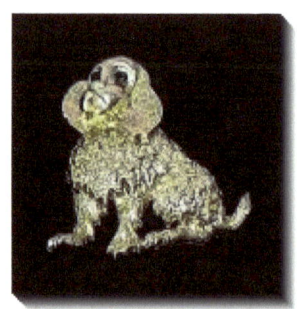
A gold plated handmade brooch.

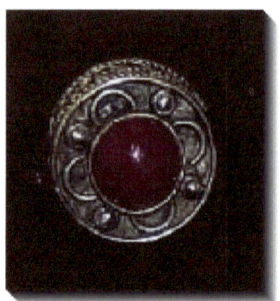

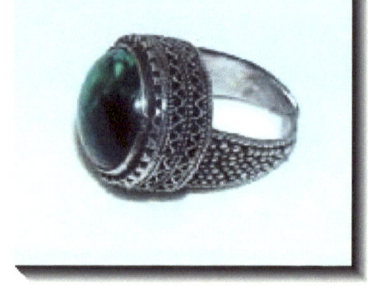

Vintage Israeli sterling silver filigree handmade rings.

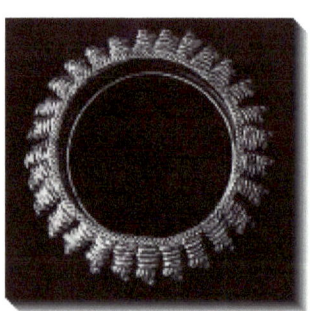
A hand made ethnic silver bracelet.

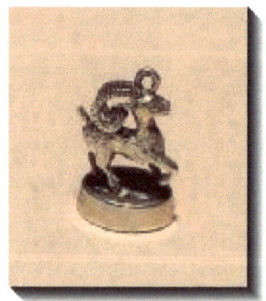
The Ram - sterling silver pendant.

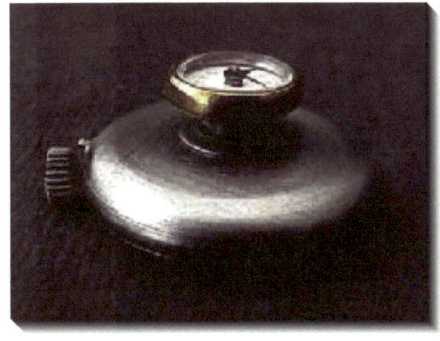 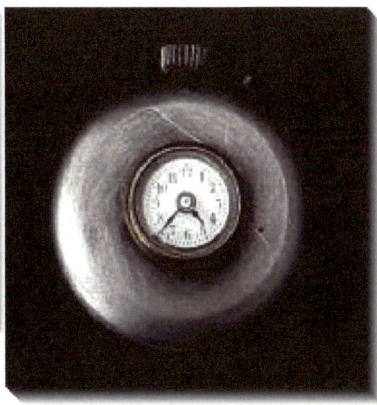

'Knob Watch', known as a *'pin set or nail set buttonhole watch'*.

This is a rare late 19th Century Swiss ball watch with small white enamel dial and black Arabic numerals, black steel case.

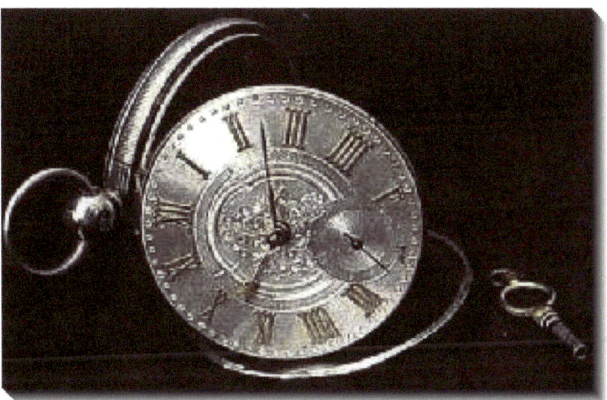

Silver cased, Fusee movement, gold and silver face, with key.
A large 19th Century English Fusee cylinder in a silver consular case.
Full plate fire gilt movement with signed dust cover, round pillars.
Attractive engine turned silver dial with applied gold Roman numerals,
the center engraved with a decorative foliate design, gilt hands.
Substantial plain silver open face case with dust proof shuts,
the gilt dust cover forming the inner cuvette.

17. Flatware and Kitchenware

Here we have a diversified collection of metal made items such as: pitchers, pots, flatware, hollow ware and general metal collectables, some made of sterling silver, silver plated, pewter and other metallic alloys.

In this category, we have a special section for kitchenware, items we use on dining tables such as: salts and condiments, napkin rings, serving flatware, tongs, ladles and tea related items.

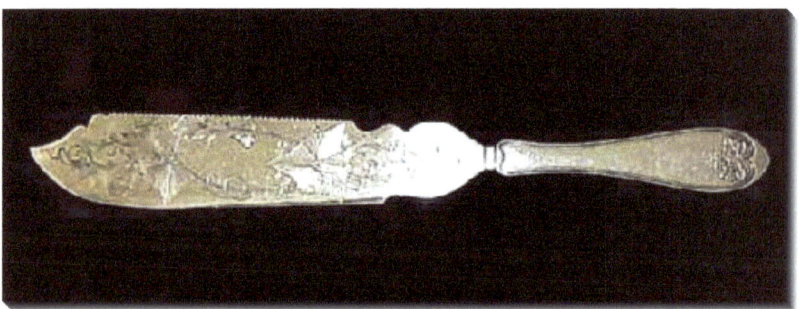

A 19C high quality server/cake/fish knife.

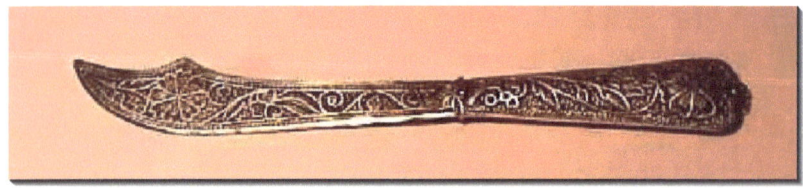

A gorgeous and rare 19C silver filigree knife.

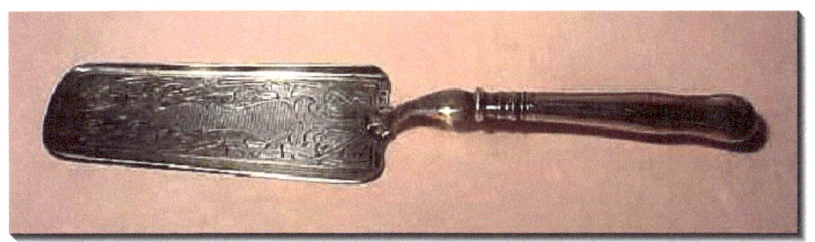

A very rare gorgeous 19C Austro-Hungarian cake server, by the famous maker **Joseph Reiner** (1822-1867).

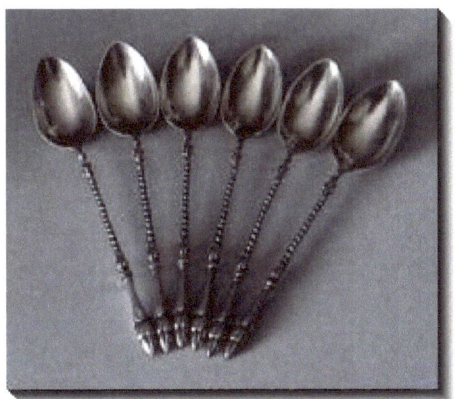 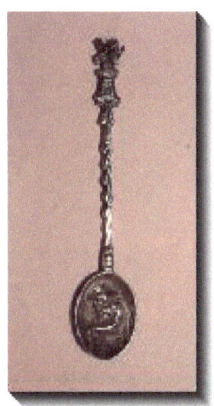

A rare set of Austro-Hungarian silver spoons.   A 19C Dutch silver spoon.

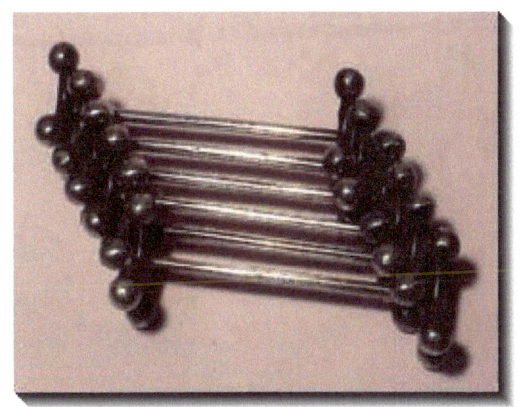

A very rare set of 6 knife rests made by Norblin, Poland during the 19C

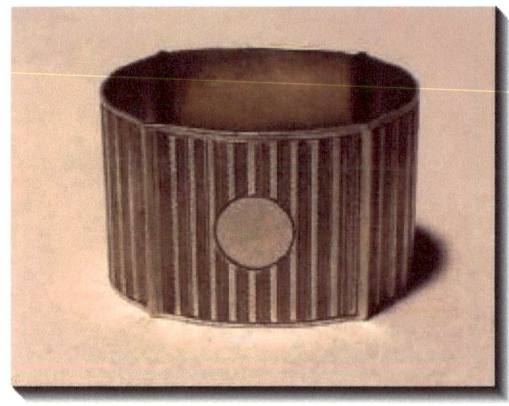

A gorgeous antique German made early 20C silver (800) napkin ring.

A gorgeous handmade sterling silver filigree napkin ring, with 5 red stones, made by a Yemenite silversmith.

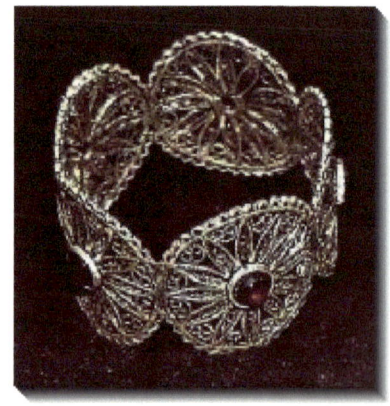

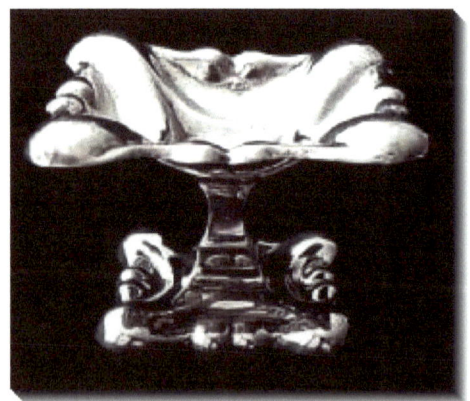

A rare Vienna Biedermeier spice dish, rectangular shape form with a lobed base and bowl. It was made in 1846 (old Vienna mark), Maker WJ Wieser Joseph 1818-54

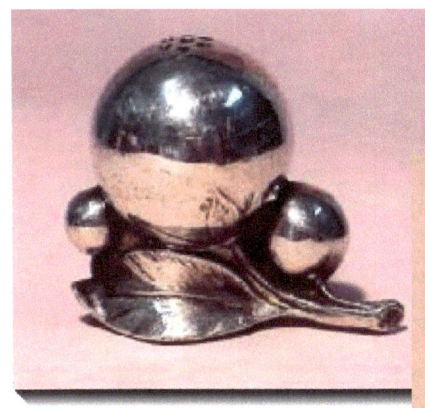
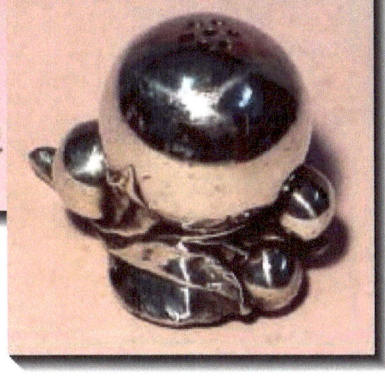

A rare art nouveau silver plated solid salt by Weidlich Brothers, marked W. B. MFG. Co. No. 64 Weidlich Brothers Mfg. Company, were manufacturing metal ware during the 1900 in Bridgeport, Connecticut.

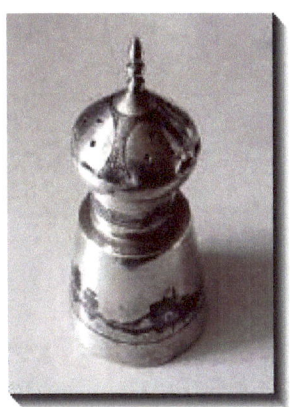
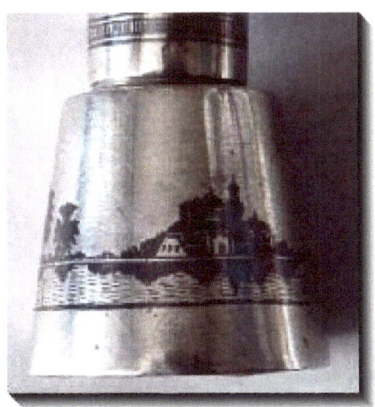

An Egyptian silver salt or spice holder with niello scenery.

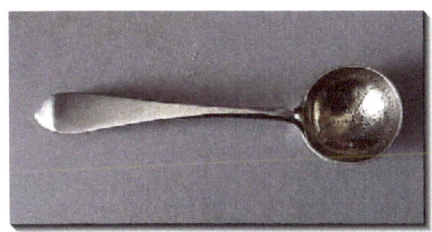
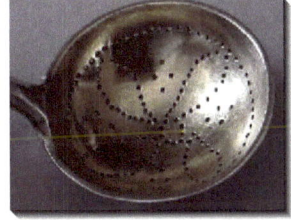

A rare 19C Polish gilded silver (12) strainer.

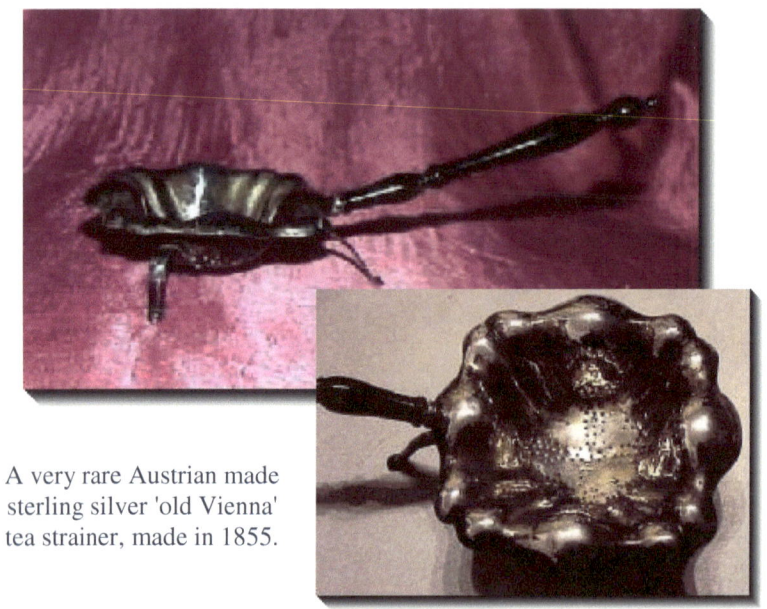

A very rare Austrian made sterling silver 'old Vienna' tea strainer, made in 1855.

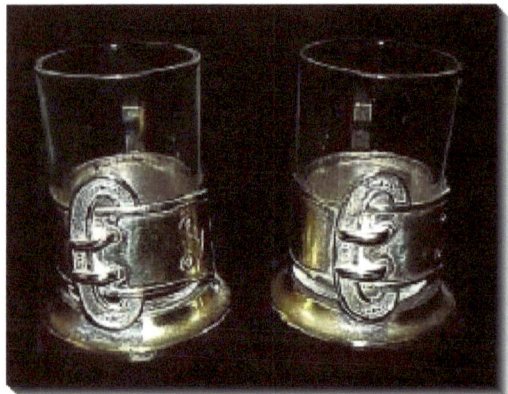

A rare pair of cup glass holders with fitted glasses, made in Poland by Norblin 19C. Marked NORBLIN & Co + GALW. + WARSZAWA, placed in the oval GALW means Galvanization.

The coat of arms of the Russian Empire (double-headed eagle) on the mark means a gold medal at the All Russia Exhibition of Manufactured Goods. The sign of the official purveyor to the Court of His Majesty Russian Tsar.

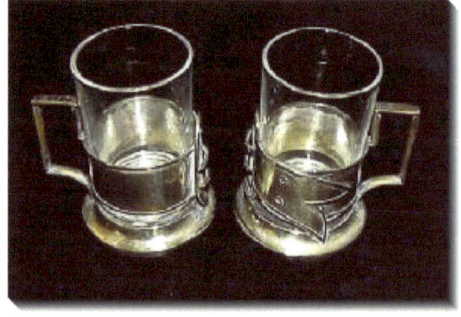

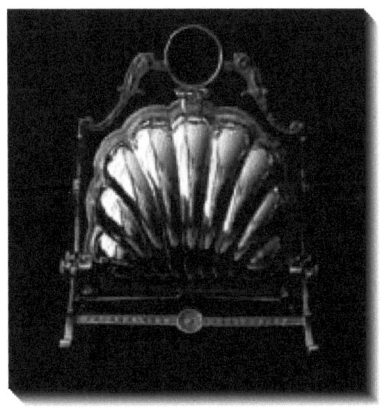 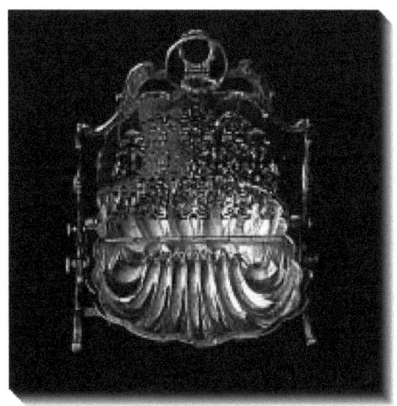

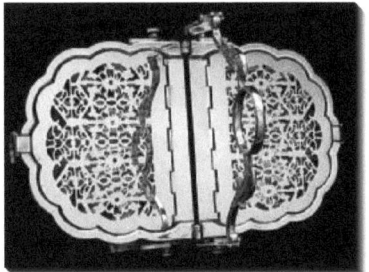 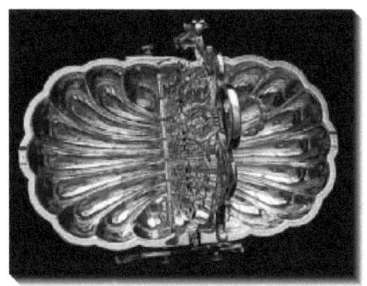

Victorian antique shell shaped folding biscuit box (muffineer)
It is a gorgeous silver plated biscuit container made about 1850-1899.

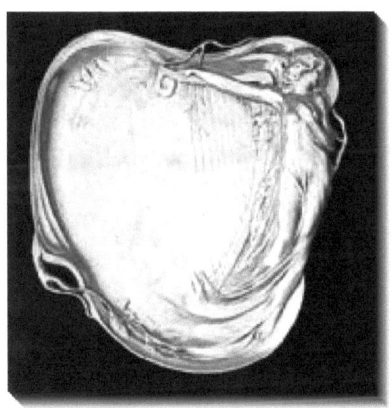 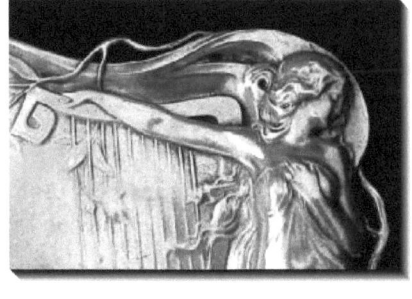

A gorgeous Art Nouveau pewter card plate.

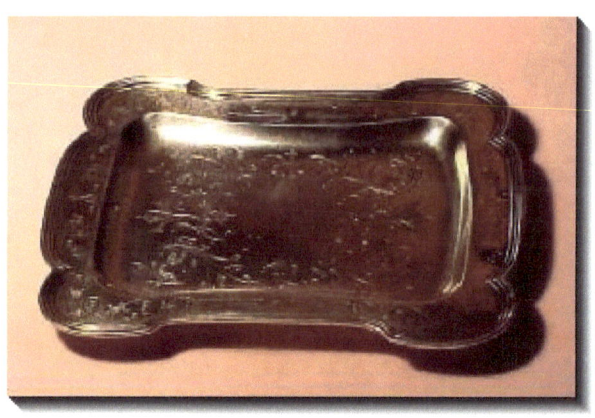

A rare Austro-Hungarian 1822 silver plate.

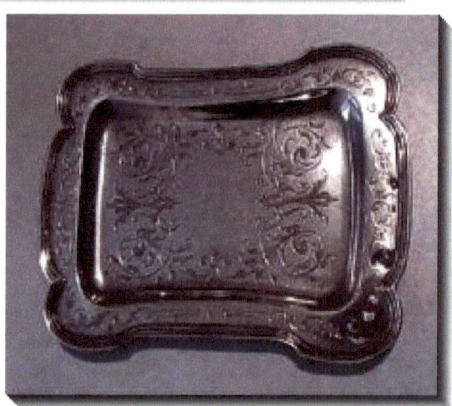

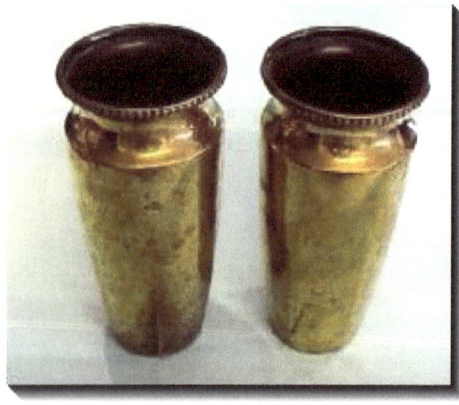
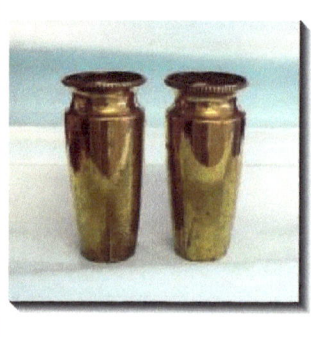

A pair of hand-beaten brass vases by WMF, Early 1900.
WMF - Württembergische Metallwarenfabrik, founded in 1853 in Geislingen an der Steige, Germany.

Two sets of large Victorian copper plates, late 19C. These plates were used as under-plates, during the Victorian era, at dinners to mark locations and protect the porcelain dinner plates.

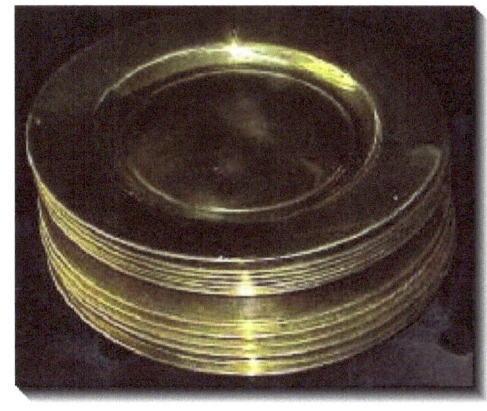

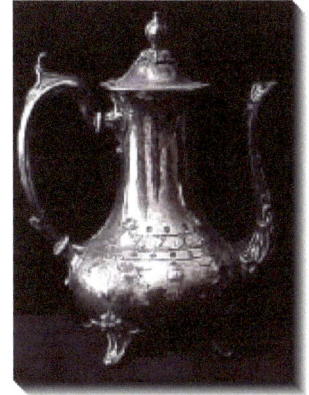

A rare Victorian tea pot, with richly embossed decoration, on 4 mask and scroll feet, signed Superior Electroplate Sheffield 1201, circa 1850.

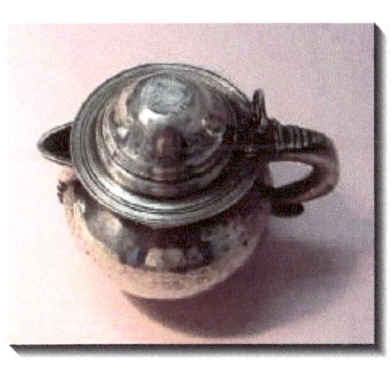

A gorgeous and rare pitcher with an antique coin from 1787 embedded An English hand hammered; maker's mark is a Menorah.

It was manufactured by Barker Bros. Silver Co., Inc. Mary Barker started this company in Birmingham, England, circa 1801.

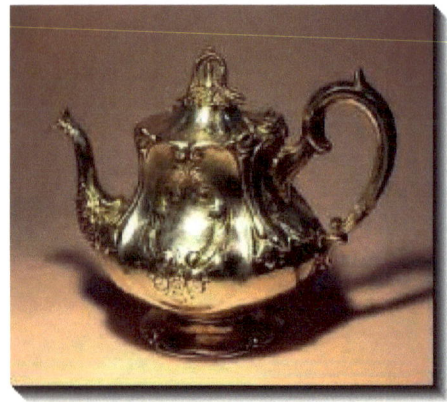 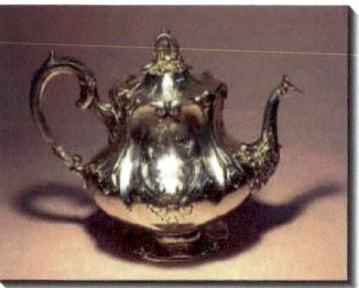

A gorgeous and rare Victorian tea pot.

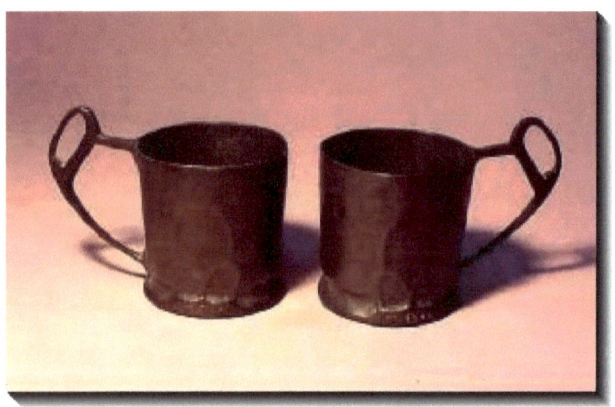

A pair of rare tea glass holders, made by Kayserzinn in 1902-1904, marked Kayserzinn 4519 in a circular stamp. The designer is Hugo Leven,

In 1862, Düsseldorf based Kayser family (J.P. Kayser & Sohn were active until 1925), opened a new factory, where they manufactured designer's items using a special lead-free alloy of tin and silver. At the world exhibitions in Paris (1900), Turin (1902), Düsseldorf and St. Louis (1904), the company enjoyed great success with its "Kayserzinn" ("Kayser pewter"). Their main designer and artistic director was **Hugo LEVEN (1874-1956).**

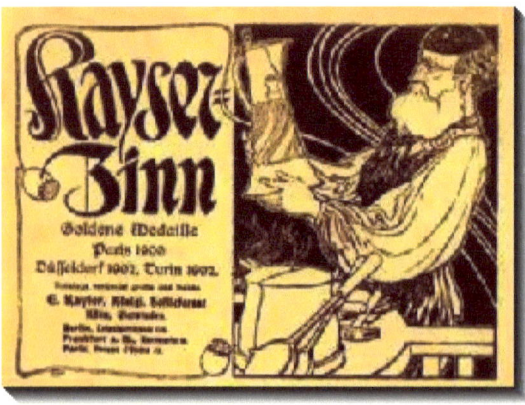

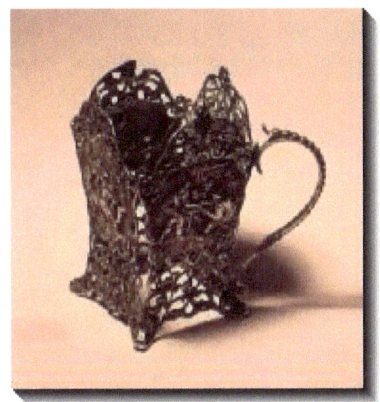 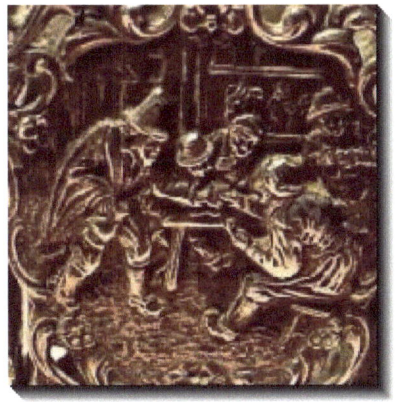

A sterling silver cup glass holder made in Holland in 1933, with gorgeous piercing and pictures.

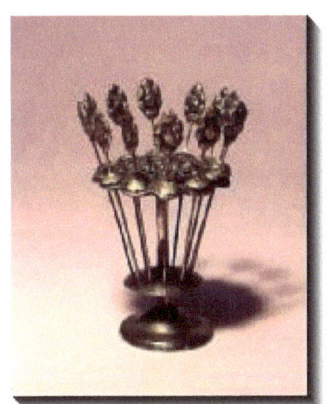

A rare set of twelve silver marked 800S Dutch 19C cocktail picks.

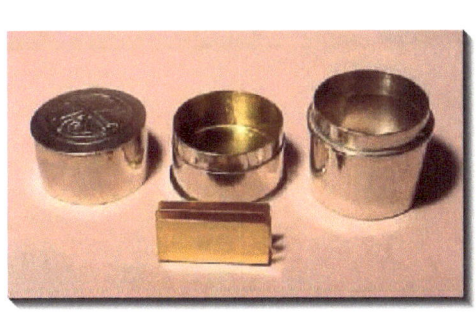 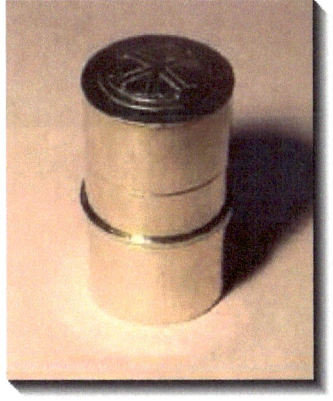

A sterling silver Communion set; all four parts hallmarked London 1954.

A Victorian folding corkscrew

A corkscrew made by Hakuli, Israel 1950s.

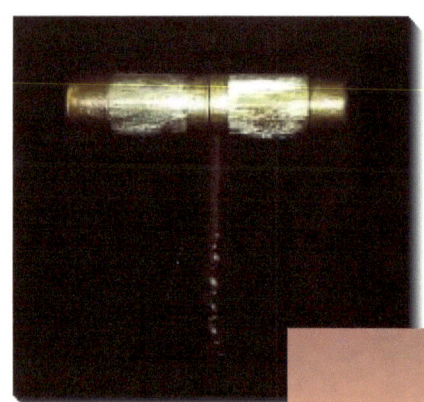

A bottle opener made by Hakuli, Israel 1950s.

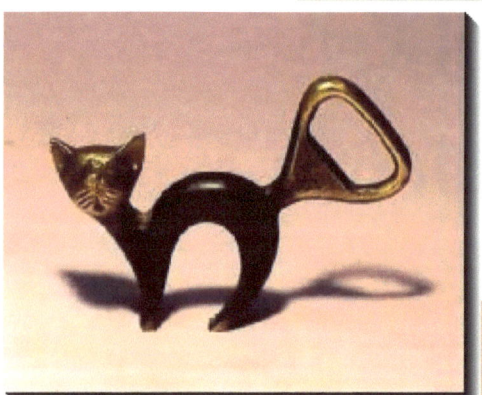

A vintage BOJ arrow owl face. Lever corkscrew.

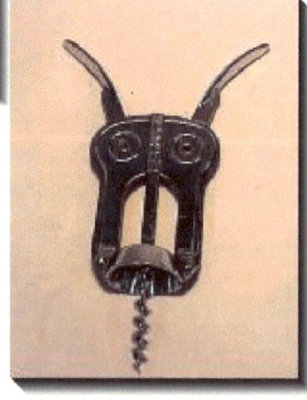

18. Paintings, Prints and Photography

Paintings, prints, lithographs, etchings, engravings and drawings are displayed in this category of art.

In addition, unique antique Tintypes – Ferrotype photographs starting from the 1860s and Carte De Visite - CDV from the 1870s are also displayed.

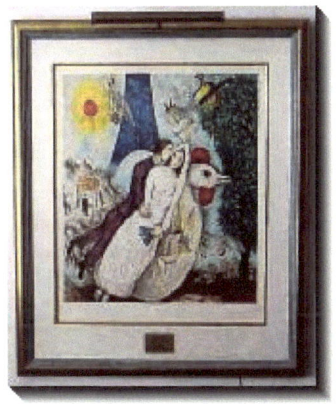

Marc Chagall, 1887-1985
The Bride and Groom of the Eiffel Tower, original lithography by Mourlot, signed and authorized by Chagall's estate, 575/750
89 cm x 102 cm

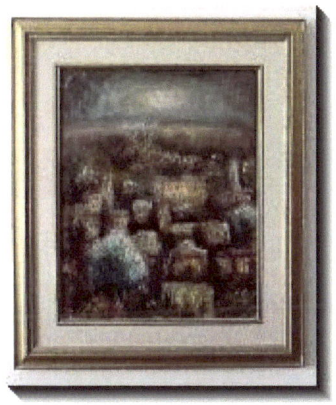

Albert Goldman, 1922-2011
Original, View of Jerusalem,
Oil on canvas.
72 cm x 80 cm

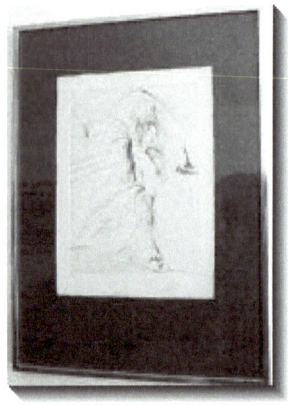 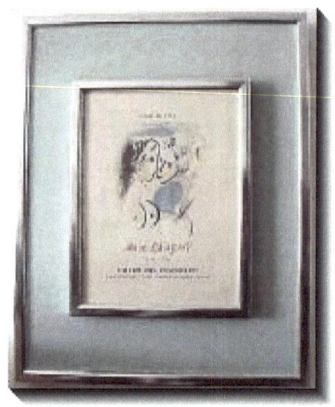

Salvador Dali, 1904-1989
Les Aigrettes (The Egrets)
from Venus aux fourrures 1969
"The Lady with Whip", a rare
original etching , signed by
Dali, 31/50; 47 cm x 62 cm

Marc Chagall, 1887-1985
Ville De Nice,
Colored Lithography,
Plate signed. (1958)
45 cm x 51 cm

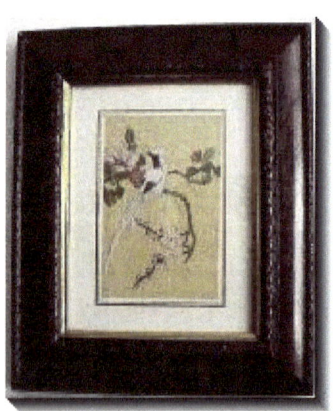 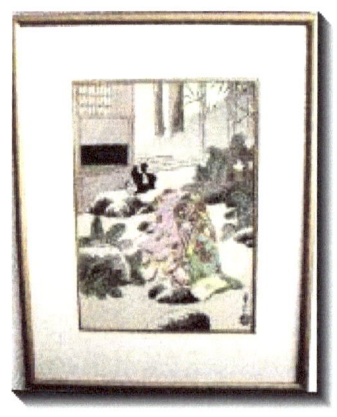

Japanese watercolor on silk
background circa 1920.
36 cm x 31 cm

An original Japanese woodblock,
Printing by the famous Uchida Art, Kyoto.
31 cm x 38.5 cm

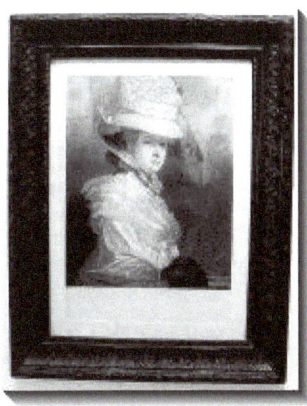 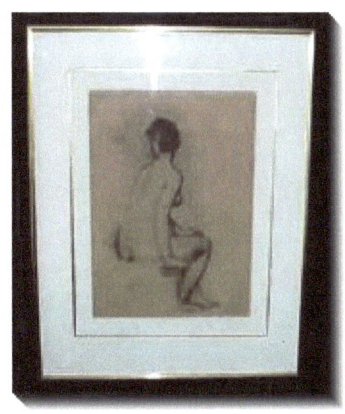

The Lady, Antique original etching.
Antique Victorian frame
46 cm x 56 cm

Renoir, A beautiful print
Paris, plate signed.
23 cm x 30 cm

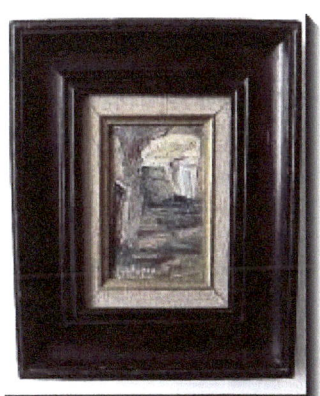 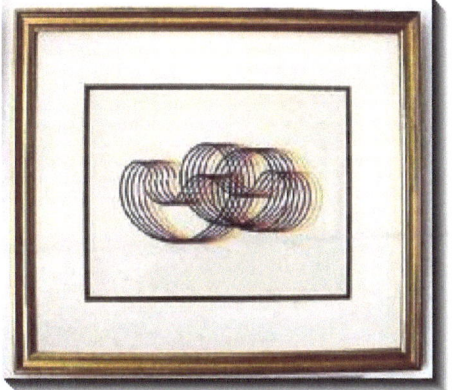

Rika Schwimer,
Streets of Zefad,
Oil painting, signed.
26 cm x 30 cm

Yaacov Agam, 1928 - ,
Colored shapes, original signed
lithography H.C.
51 cm x 43 cm

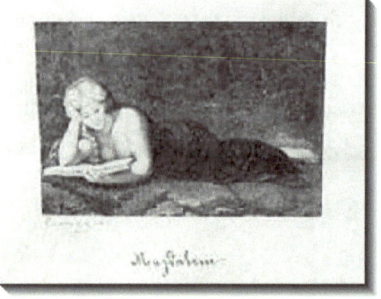
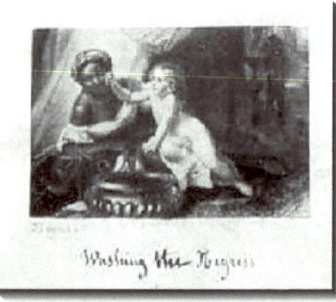
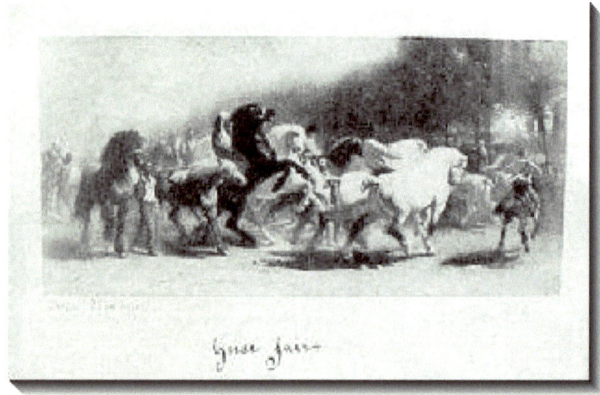
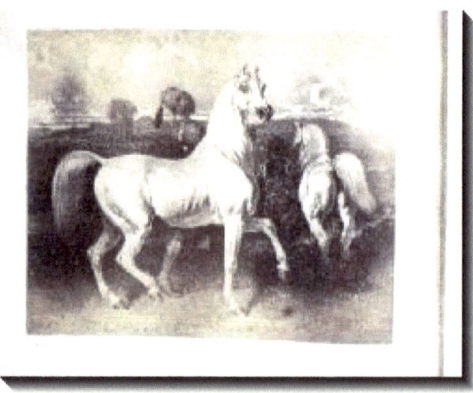

Four rare antique etching/engraving, England, c. 1860. 28 x 31 cm

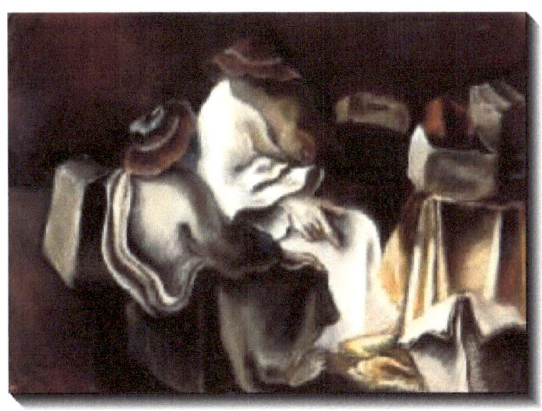

Sarit Gura, B. Tel-Aviv, 1952 - , original, signed, 84 x 66 cm

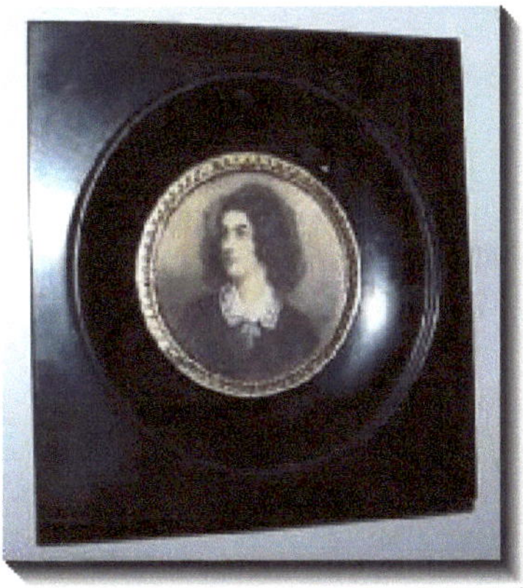

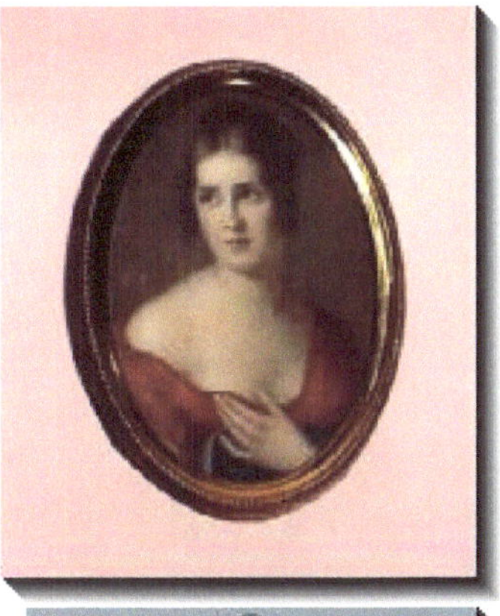

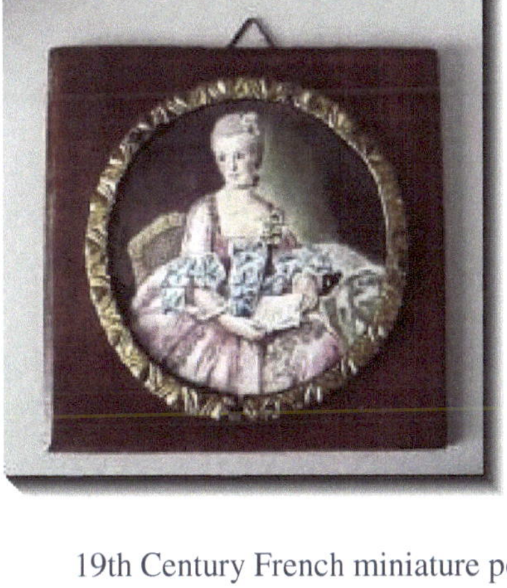

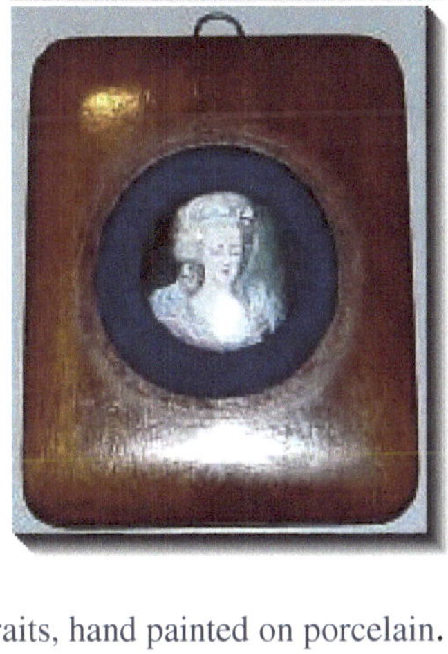

19th Century French miniature portraits, hand painted on porcelain.

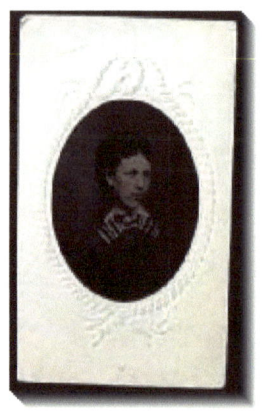
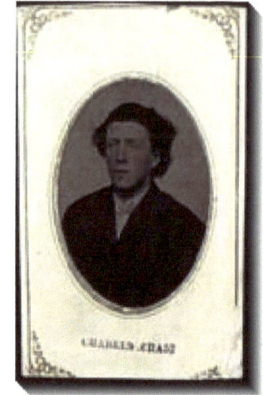
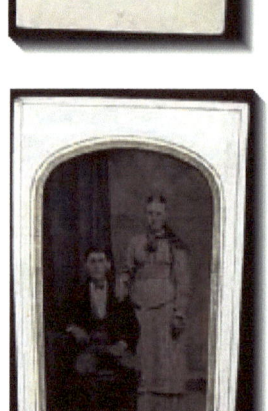
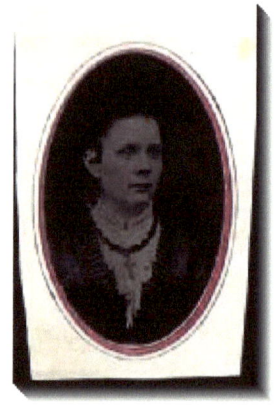

Tintype and ferrotype, started in the 1850s, is a photograph made by creating a direct positive on a sheet of iron metal that is blackened by painting.

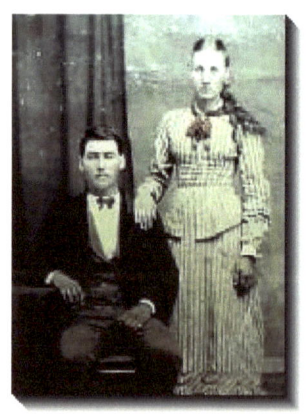

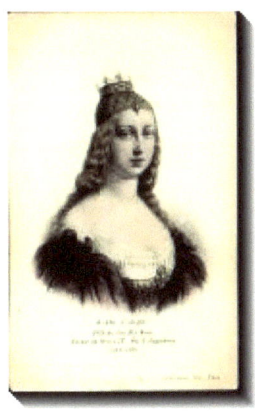
Marie d'Anjou

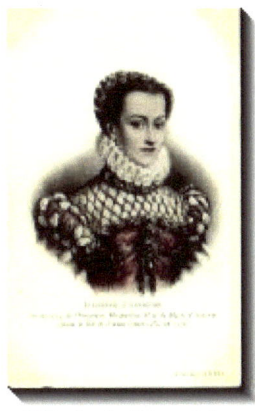
Elisabeth d'Autriche

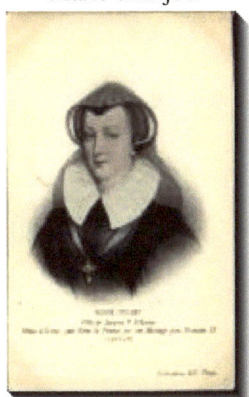
Marie Stuart

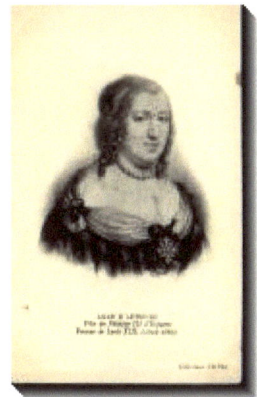
Anne d'Autriche

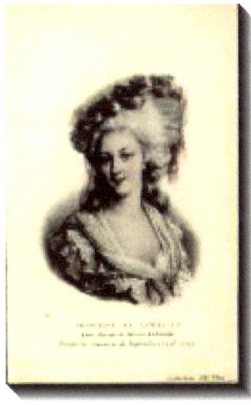
Princesse De Lamballe

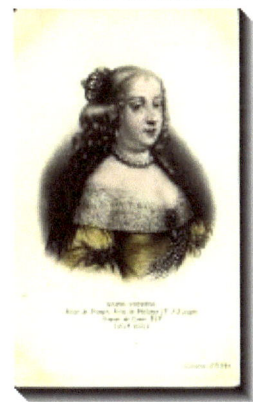
Marie Thérèse

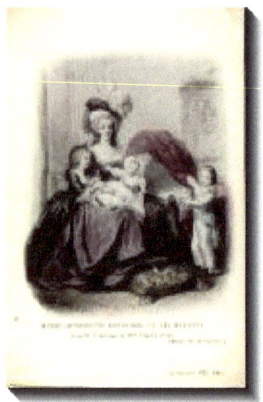 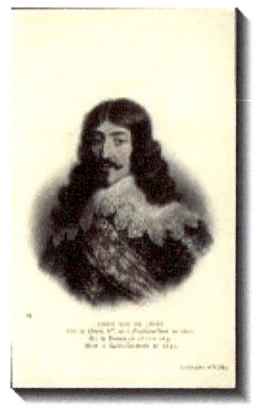

       Marie Antoinette   Louis XIII le Juste

All postcards above were made by ND Phot in Paris, France, early 1900.

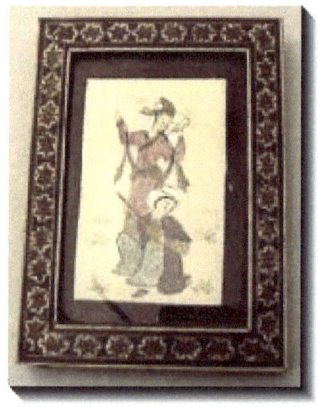

A 19th Century Persian miniature hand painting on Faux Ivory.
Framed in a Khatam style. 12 x 16 cm

19. Asian Art

Asian art in this chapter includes Japanese *Inro*, *Netsuke*, Ivory and other sculptures made in Japan and China.

Inrō were most commonly used to carry identity seals, money, tobbaco and medicine as the traditional Japanese garb or *kimono* had no pockets. The inrō consisted of a stack of small nested boxes. The boxes were held together by a rope or cord, the end of the cord was secured or toggled to a netsuke. A bead or ojime was used between the inrō and the netsuke to hold the boxes.

Netsuke in Japanese means "(ne) root" and "(tsuke) to attach". It is a small sculpture that was carved usually in ivory since the seventeenth century in Japan.

It is rather difficult to photo a Netsuke, in reality they are much more impressive. A close-up photo of such a small item (about 2"-3") shows the high quality and details of the carving.

As they were carved from various parts of different types of real ivory, the color varies, some are darker and some are whiter.

Those ivory art works were acquired from prominent and reliable antique dealers, through auctions worldwide. They were carved from ivory, some time between the end of 19th Century and early 20th Century, but definitely before 1945.

According to DEFRA (Department for Environment, Food and Rural Affairs), as they were made pre 1947, there is no need for a certificate to sell according to article 10.

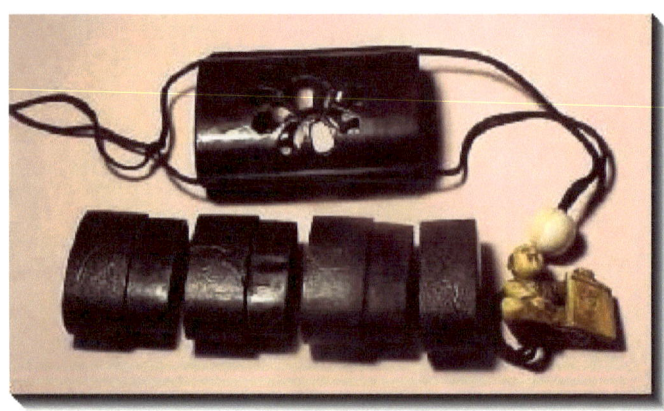

A rare set of Inro from the Meiji period (1860-1910), with Ojime and Netsuke.

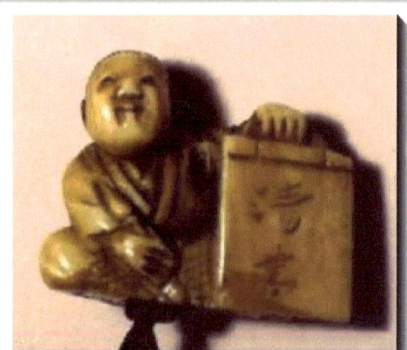

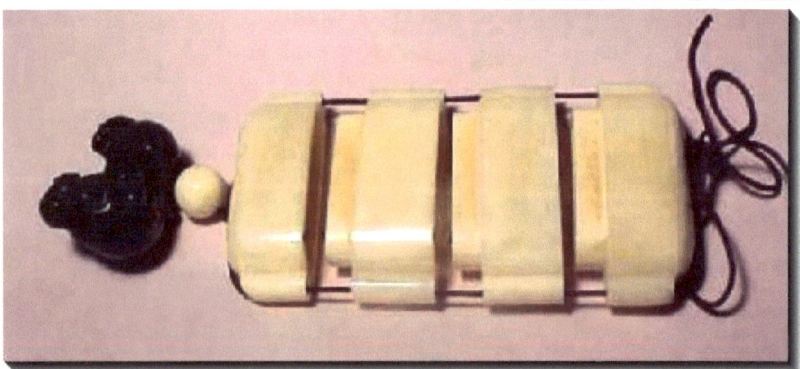

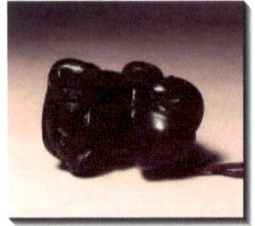

A unique black and white Inro set, early 20C. The inro is 4 compartments made of bone, the ojime from ivory. The netsuke is very detailed and carved from ironwood.

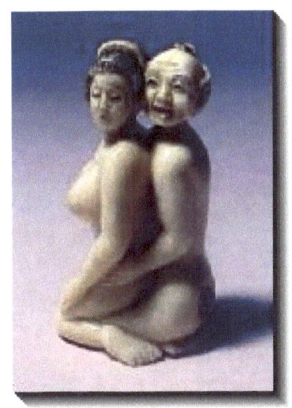

Erotic elephant ivory netsuke, very detailed carving, early 20C, master artist signed.

The tsuba is a guard at the end of the grip of Japanese sword, mainly to be used to prevent the hand from sliding onto the blade during thrusts.

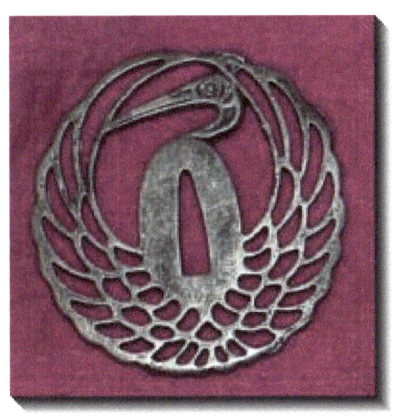

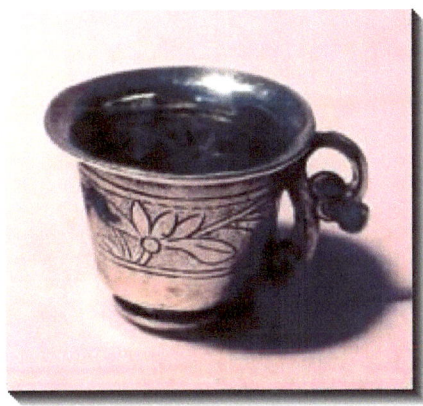

This is a very fine Qing dynasty small wine cup. The Chinese traditionally drank two kinds of native drinks called Mao Tai Jiu and Bai Jiu. This is a type of cup that would have been used during important gatherings.

It is made entirely of silver, and partially enameled. It has a nice design on it and a handle. This is a very rare and authentic item.

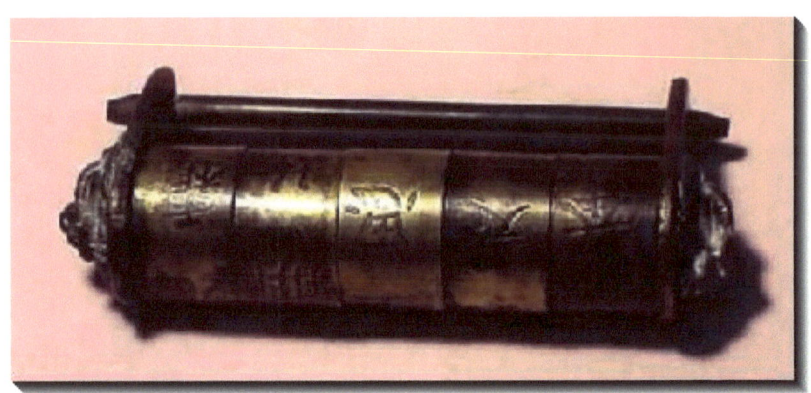

A beautiful authentic antique Chinese lock The Chinese characters on the lock are: "Reminiscent to homeland."

This poem was written by the famous Tang dynasty poet "Li-Bai" when he was away from home.
Lǐ Bái was born in 701 in Shanxi province and died in 762.

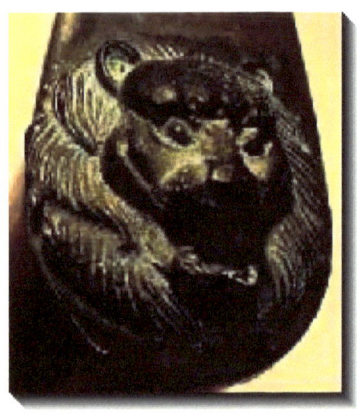

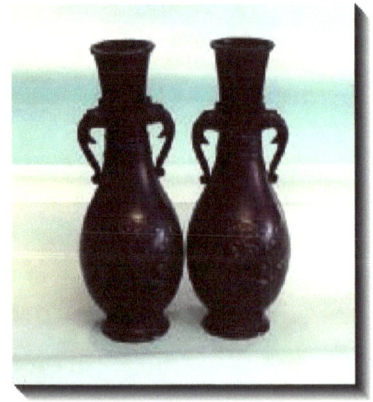

A pair of 19C Meiji period Japanese bronze vases.

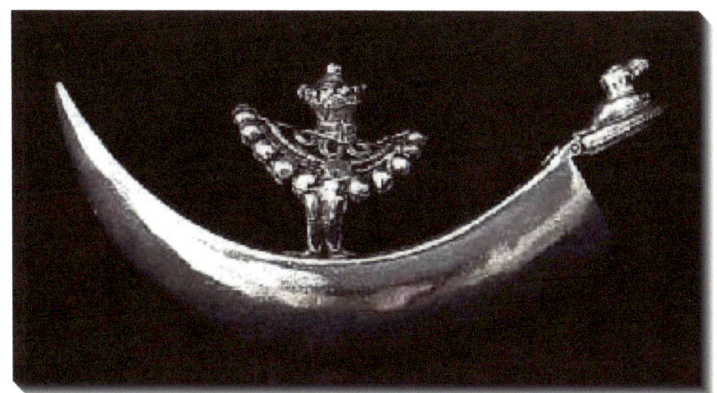

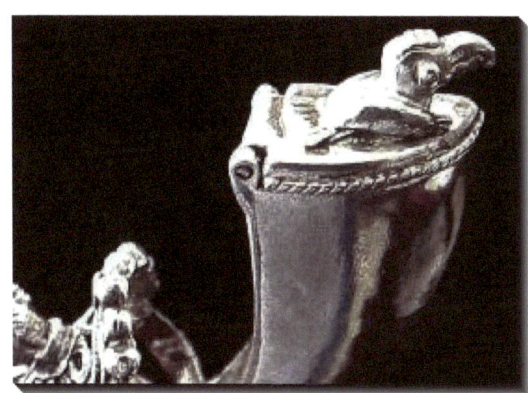

An unusual and rare container, probably for gun-powder use. It is made of a high silver-content zinc alloy; a bird-like artwork is functioning as a cover.

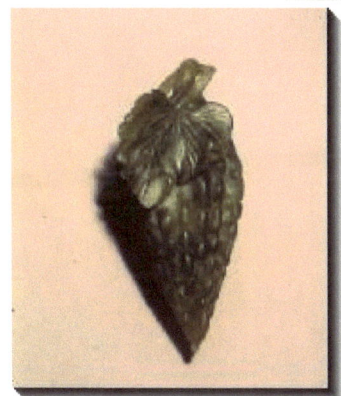
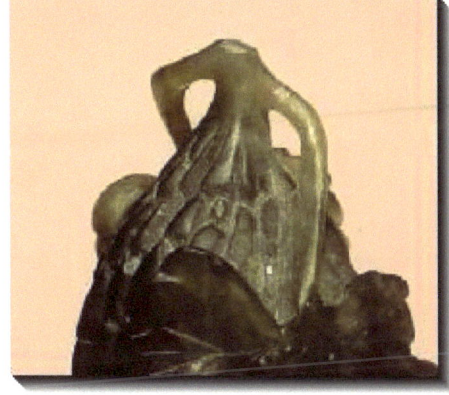

A 19C Chinese large jade, gorgeous carving.

20. Furniture, Carpets and Lighting

Antique and vintage furniture are displayed with carpets, rugs and lighting ware.

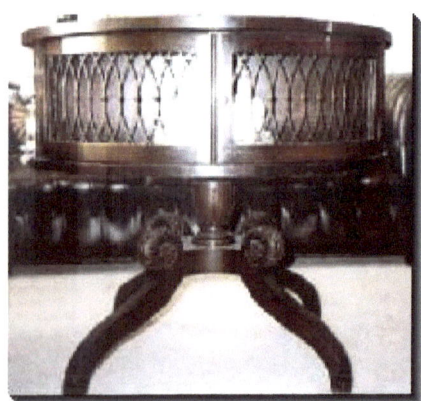

An early American mahogany round table with leather inlaid top on 4 carved legs.

A pair of 'his&hers' arm chairs, with red velvet upholstery, carved frame Cabriole legs, circa 1890.

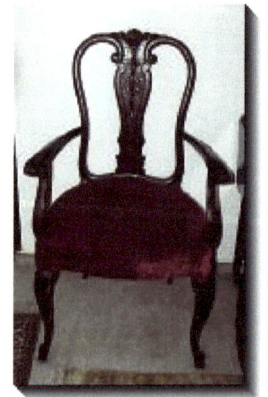 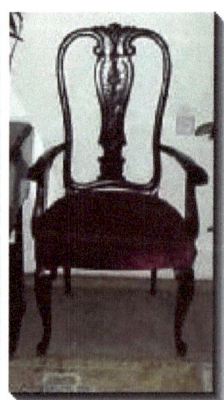

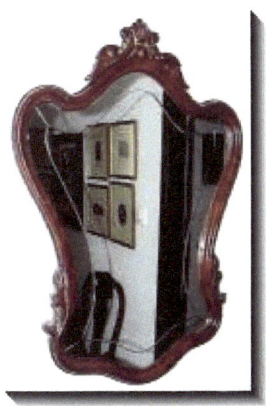

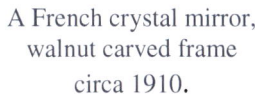

A French crystal mirror, walnut carved frame circa 1910.

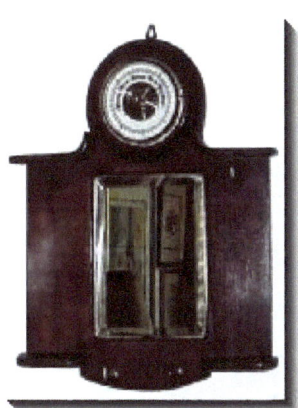

A rare original 19C ship's Barometer with crystal mirror.

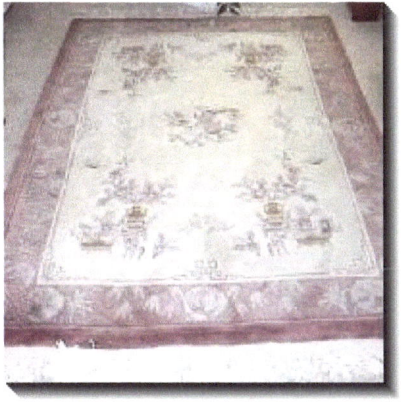

Hand knotted and hand carved super 90 line 5/8" pile, 100% pure wool pile, made in China. (196X135 cm)

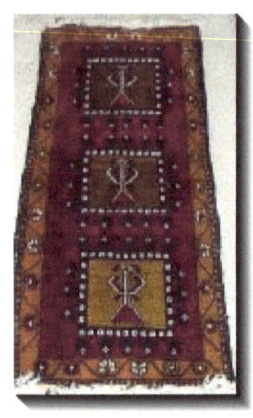

A unique Persian 19C
praying carpet.
(45 x 94 cm)

A Pakistani 'runner',
pattern on pink background carpet
(312X78 cm).

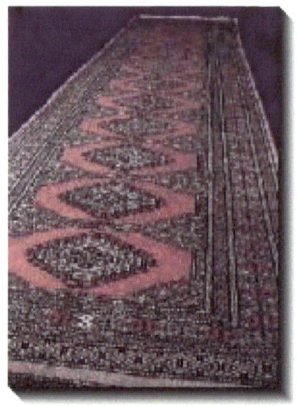

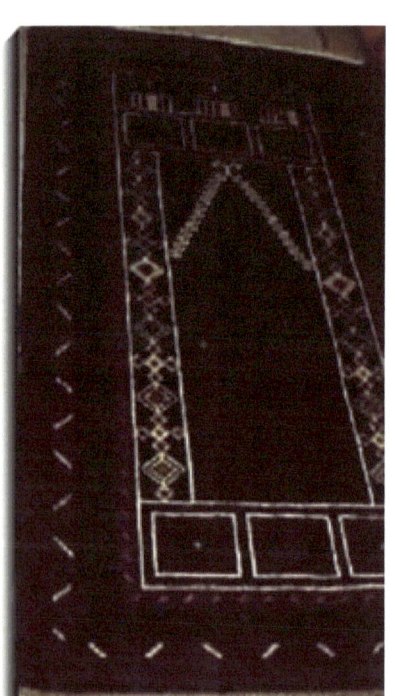

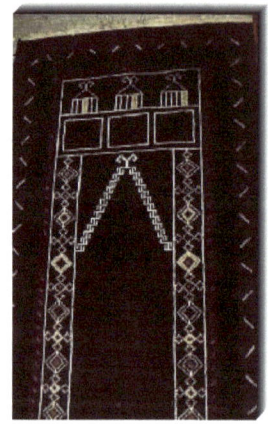

A Persian Balouch,
(88 x 157 cm)

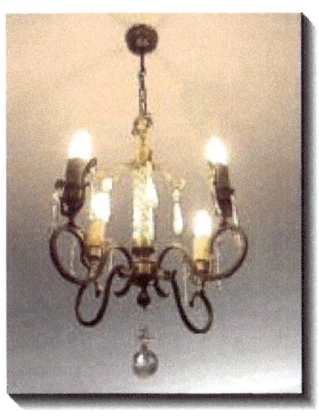

A French bronze chandelier,
Four arms with crystal dripstones,
circa 1910 (restored by the author).

A French bronze double arm
'appliqué' lamps,
circa 1930.

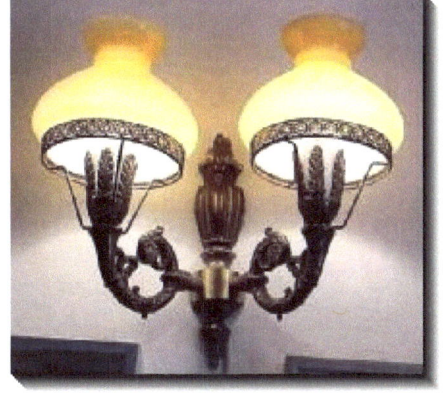

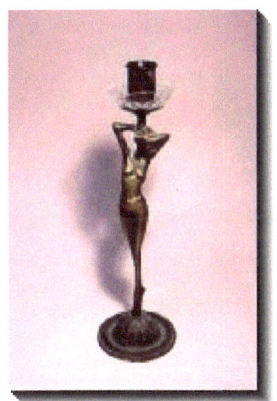

A beautiful Art-Nouveau style
bronze lamp.

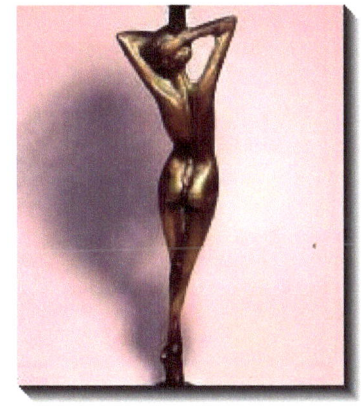

21. General Antiques and Collectables

In this last chapter, a few more findings and general suggestions are given for existing and potential collectors.

Before you decide to purchase, or bid on an item, you should ask yourself two questions:

Does this item 'speak' to me and can I afford it.

The item you pick, either for your own collection, or for resale, should be one that you like. You will bring it to your home; you'll have to live with it, especially if it is a large item such as furniture. In this case, it is desired to consult with your spouse or family prior the purchase. You might develop an antagonistic feeling toward an object that generated a family dispute.

About the price of an item, you may consider the possibility for resale if you are a dealer, or for your own collection.

Obviously, there are more possibilities, such as donation or gift, but my idea is that you should not get a mortgage or a loan to finance the purchase of an expensive item.

The negotiation phase is important, not only to reduce the price, but also for your own good feeling. This is especially important if you consider resale.

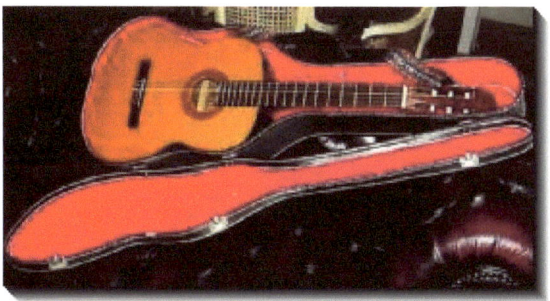

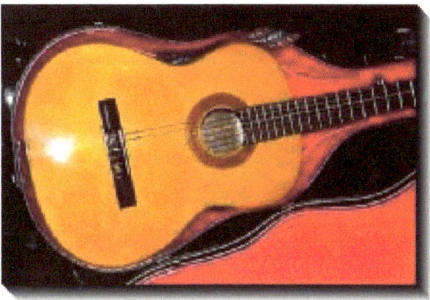

An American made 6 string classical guitar with case, circa 1960s. Model 7097-B Original Ace Guitar Strap (like Hendrix used at Woodstock).

While living in the US, I bought this guitar in New Jersey from a guy who claimed to attend Woodstock in August 1969. He had the right look and needed the money. Since then, I have replaced the strings and it is in perfect condition. I was unable to identify the real maker of this model (Model 7097-B).

I bought a few interesting items in garage sales in the New Jersey and New York area. One of them was actually not for sale as the owner did not think anybody would pay anything for it, as it was broken with missing parts piled in his garage.

It was an old gramophone by Aeolian Vocalion. After paying just a few dollars, I spent many lovely weekends in restoring it to its glory. I found the missing parts and after some handy work on the entire furniture housing, I was thrilled when I played it for the first time.

The volume control is really fun. It is done by using a long cable which controls the volume by opening and closing the 'sound hole'.

To increase or decrease the volume, I have to hold the long outer black sleeve in one hand and pull or push the knob with the other to change the volume.

This rare original Phonograph made in the early 20th century is housed in its original mahogany music stand case, with a variable speed control. It has an internally based conical horn. Below the player there are cabinet shelves for storing records. It plays a nostalgic original sound from the early 20th century.

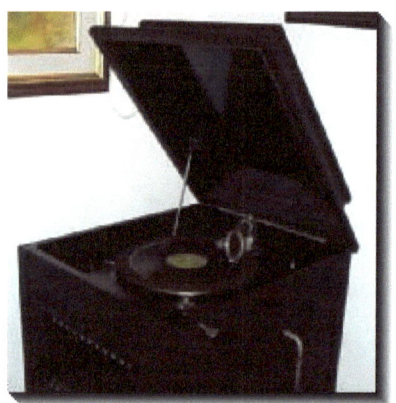

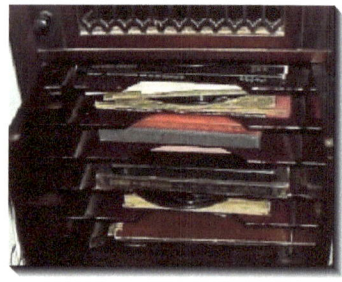

A Gramophone, 1916-20
by Aeolian Vocalion
Graduola
(S.N. 430-1, Style-400)

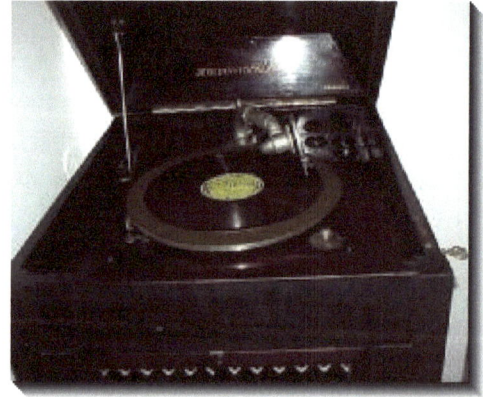

Another exciting adventure was when I bought an old violin at Newark Fair in the north of England, with no strings or bridge, and in a very poor condition. I loved the shape and the price…

Looking carefully inside the box I discovered a note saying:

Antonius Stradivarius Cremonensis Faciebat Anno 1689

Obviously, I was excited. In London, I took it to one of the professional restorers, who pulled me back to the ground…

He explained that it was a generic name for violins. Although mine is obviously not a Stradivarius, it was made in Germany about 150 years ago. It has a nice body worthy of restoring, which I did. He made a great job of it and I was still excited when he played it for me for the first time.

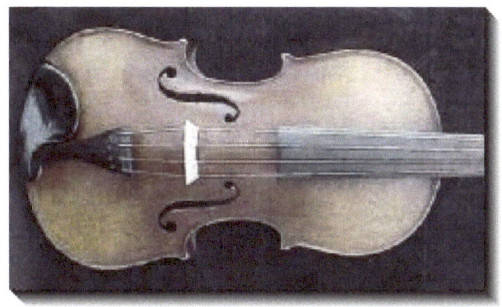

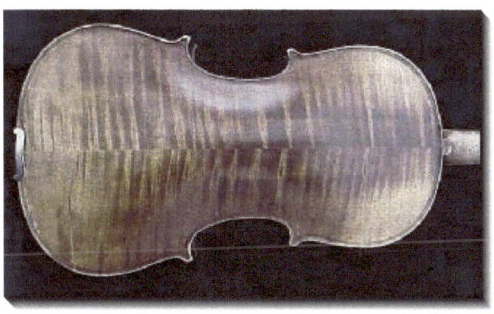

A 'Stradivarius' Violin made in 1689…

Warwick vase, fine details, heavy bronze.

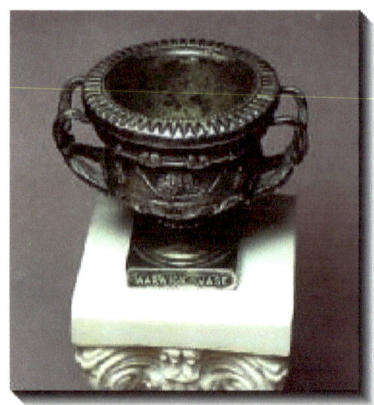

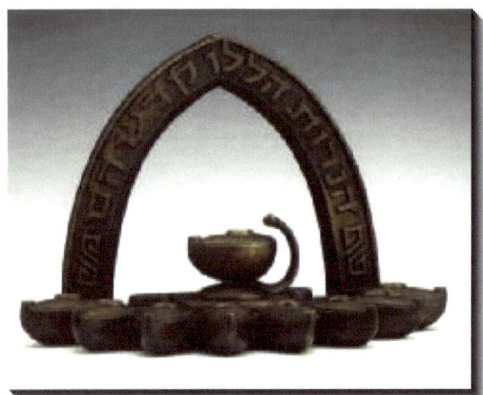

A Menorah-Hanukkah lamp by Pal-Bell 1950s.

A Victorian bronze inkwell.

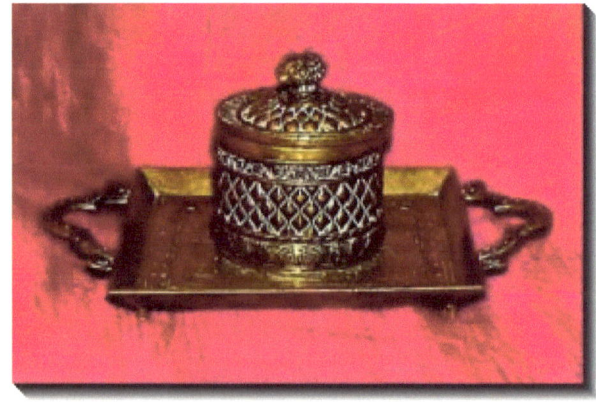

A rare small Austrian bronze figurine, circa 1910.

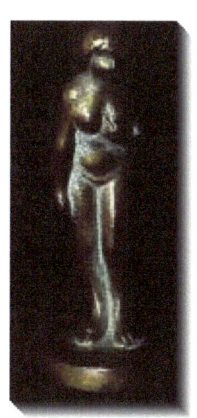

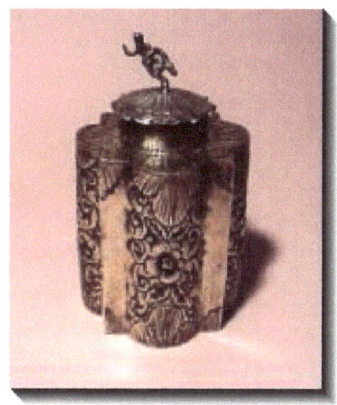

A silver 19C tea caddy.

A dancer, bronze Israel 1950s.

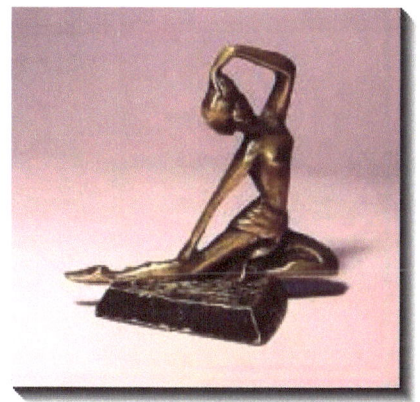

22. Epilogue

The philosophical negotiations and objects selected to be displayed in this book were based on the author's experience and personal interests, as touched on in the prologue.

Each of the objects is described in detail, as far as possible, on the website of the *Antiques Online Catalogue*. Extensive literature is available for those who wish to deepen their knowledge and interest in the specific objects described.

About the author: Giora speaks Hungarian, Hebrew, English and German; his hobbies are antiques and collectables, painting and wood carvings.

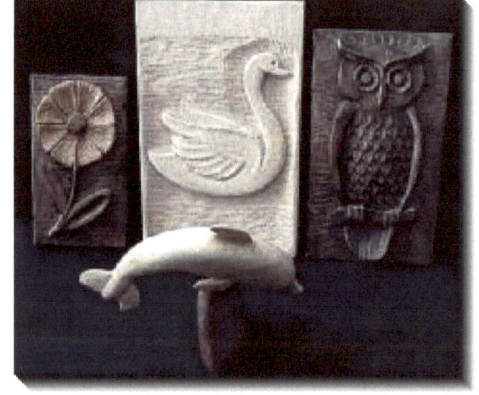

Wood carving 'creations' by the author.

I hope that you will find what you are looking for.

www.ingramcontent.com/pod-product-compliance
Lightning Source LLC
Chambersburg PA
CBHW040217220526
45473CB00001B/18